SECOND EDITION

42 Rules for Sensible Investing (2ⁿᵈ Edition)

A Practical, Entertaining and Educational Guidebook for Personal Investment Strategies

By Leon Shirman

∫UPER∫taR
press

E-mail: info@superstarpress.com
20660 Stevens Creek Blvd., Suite 210
Cupertino, CA 95014

Published by Super Star Press™, a Happy About® imprint
20660 Stevens Creek Blvd., Suite 210, Cupertino, CA 95014
http://42rules.com

2nd Edition: November 2012
1st Edition: December 2008
Paperback ISBN (2nd Edition): 978-1-60773-112-2 (1-60773-112-6)
Paperback ISBN (1st Edition): 978-1-60773-008-8 (1-60773-008-1)
eBook ISBN: 978-1-60773-009-5 (1-60773-009-X)
Place of Publication: Silicon Valley, California, USA
Library of Congress Number: 2008940963

Trademarks

Warning and Disclaimer

Praise For This Book!

"This book condenses enough wisdom into these 42 straightforward rules to save investors years of learning through costly experiences."
Abbott J. Keller, CFA
Chief Investment Officer
Kestrel Investment Management Corporation

"42 Rules for Sensible Investing is a clear, easy to read, objective and balanced review of the basic fundamentals of investing. It is ideal and essential for the novice and a helpful reminder for the experienced investor."
Bert Frydman, Author and Consultant
Former Chairman of the Board
Valley Credit Union

"The book provides a great summary of investment techniques in concise and understandable form. A must read for anyone who doesn't have time to go through voluminous tomes on investing."
Vieta Rosenberg, CPA
Profit Factor

"Valuable and actionable advice for both novice and experienced investors delivered in enjoyable and easy to read manner."
Bryan Koffman
General Partner
PanTerra Investments

Publisher

- Mitchell Levy
  http://superstarpress.com/ and http://happyabout.com/

Executive Editor

- Laura Lowell
  http://42rules.com/

Cover Designer

- Catherine Borgen
  http://seebedesign.com/

Layout

- Teclarity
  http://teclarity.com/

Dedication

To Lilia, for her boundless optimism and steadfast belief in my abilities.

"Live long and prosper"

Traditional greeting of Vulcans, who, by virtue of living by logic and reason, without interference from emotion, must be very good investors.

Contents

Contents

Just as I have completed the first draft of this book, the markets experienced their worst week ever (October 6–10, 2008), with the S&P 500 falling by 18%. The indices are down over 40% from their latest peak reached almost exactly one year ago. We are in the midst of the greatest financial crisis since the Great Depression. What a time to be writing a book on investing!

These are certainly very scary times. Banks, suffering from massive write-offs related to the collapse of mortgage-based securities, are hoarding their cash and are reluctant to lend. If banks don't lend, businesses can't finance their daily operations and could be forced to shut down. And this being a worldwide crisis, the economy of the whole world is in serious jeopardy. That is why governments across the world are taking action to inject trillions of dollars into the banking system to prevent an economic meltdown. It is not clear at this point how successful these actions will be.

Today's events are clearly unprecedented and terrifying. But let's take a look at the previous three major bear markets. From 2000 through 2002, the market fell 45%. This was the time when hundreds of high tech companies were going out of business, erasing trillions of market value. The events of 9/11 that happened during this period were also unprecedented and terrifying. No one was sure whether we would ever feel safe at home again.

On October 19, 1987, the market fell 23% in a single day. That was the worst day loss ever, both in point and percentage terms at the time, worse than the crash that marked the beginning of the Great Depression. That was unprecedented and terrifying, and there were many doomsday predictions of markets falling much further. It didn't happen. In 1973–1974, the market fell 48%. We had double-digit inflation and unemployment rates, and our oil supply was choked off by the Arab embargo. That, also, was unprecedented and terrifying.

Each major bear market is unique and frightening in its own way, and it seems that the world is about to end...again. But the economy and the markets recovered from each of these setbacks, and proceeded their march to new highs. I have reason to believe that this will be the case this time, too.

When I was writing this book, I, like everybody else, did not imagine that we were about to witness these calamitous days. Other than adding examples, however, I am not planning to make modifications to the book. The investing principles presented here still apply in the current situation, perhaps even more so. The events of the last several weeks, as historic as they may have been, will not change my long-term investing philosophy and the Rules for Sensible Investing.

Leon Shirman

October 13, 2008

For obvious reasons, the topic of investing is a very popular one. Countless volumes are available on many investing aspects, such as thorough analysis of past market performance, psychology of investing, stock selection, etc. Why write another book?

In *42 Rules for Sensible Investing*, I compiled practical approaches and techniques that I used over the years into a number of concise and easy-to-follow rules. The rules themselves are not new, and I am sure many people have been and are using them, either consciously or subconsciously. Some of them I arrived at by personal trial and error, some I consider to be common sense, and some were inspired by strategies used by successful investors.

I like to think of this book as a condensation of valuable investment ideas—Cliffs Notes on investing, if you will. It is not a substitution for a textbook. You will not find detailed discussions and descriptions of various methodologies here. Instead, think of it as a checklist you can refer to when you make an investment decision.

Different people can have completely different investment approaches, and still be successful. I realize and understand that. The rules presented in this book work well for me, but I don't expect you to concur with every one of them. In fact, you will probably disagree with a few. Keep this in mind when you read through the book.

I am hopeful that flipping through these rules (which you don't need to do in order) will prompt you to think about your own rules and even to write them down. Please feel free to pass these rules to others and to start a discussion. After all, these are my rules. What are yours?

1 Rules Are Meant to Be Broken

Rules can be bent, stretched, or even broken—as long as they are not yours.

Rules exist in all aspects of life. Some are always obeyed, and some are frequently broken. For example, rules in mathematics are absolute. If you don't follow them, then you are simply wrong. Rules for English language pronunciation, on the other hand, have so many exceptions that it seems that they are broken more often than they are obeyed.

What about investing? Clearly, there are no absolute rules that work and that everyone knows about. Otherwise, we would all be sitting on a beach sipping piña coladas. It is said that Warren Buffett has only two rules:

Rule #1. Never lose money.

Rule #2. Don't forget Rule #1.

Now, that's a set of rules all of us could benefit from.

The rules presented in this book are both rigid and flexible at the same time. For me, they are absolute, because they are *my* rules. I have developed them over the years, have full faith in them and follow them without hesitation. But they are not *your* rules. You are free to bend, stretch, or even throw away any rule in this book and replace it with your own. Therein lies the activeness and uniqueness of investing. It is very multifaceted—different people can be very successful while utilizing completely different strategies, techniques, and sets of rules. Hopefully this book will help you to develop yours, and, once you have your rules, follow them to the letter.

2 Compound Interest Is Good

It is amazing how each dollar invested compounds over time. The earlier you start, the more impressed you will be.

It is said that in 1609, the Dutch purchased the Manhattan Island from a native Indian tribe for an equivalent of $24 in beads and trinkets. Do you think that it was a good deal? It may certainly appear so, but yet, if they were to invest that $24 at 10% interest, after almost 400 years it would have grown to about 800 quadrillion dollars (one quadrillion is one thousand trillion, or one million billion). This should be more than enough to purchase all real estate property not only on Manhattan, but on the whole planet.

Unfortunately, we don't have four centuries to invest, but compound interest can work wonders even in our short lifetimes. The 10% rate mentioned above is a historical average return of S&P 500—the most popular benchmark for the performance of the U.S. stock market—as measured from the early 1900's. That's on average; there were and will be big up years, and well as down years. But if you have a reasonably long investment horizon, time is on your side.

Now, let's consider a more realistic example. Let's say you take $5,000 of your savings and invest it in the stock market. In 30 years, it will grow to over $87,000. This certainly beats having that money under the mattress, or in a bank savings account. Even if you don't have that $5,000 to start, maybe you can spare $200 each month from your paycheck. If you do that for 30 years, you will have about $452,000. Again, time is on your side.

Even though I have seen results like these many times, I am continually impressed. Can it be right that one can amass over $450,000 just by putting in $200 per month? Witness the power of compounding. Albert Einstein is said to have called it the most powerful principle he ever witnessed. That is a rather strong endorsement from Einstein, as he did discover a few other powerful principles as well.

The table below shows how a single investment of $10,000 grows at various rates of return compounded annually. Two percent is what you can typically get from a savings account (if you are lucky), 5% is typical CD (certificate of deposit) rate, and 10%, as discussed before, is the historical stock market average.

Year	2%	5%	10%	15%	20%
0	$10,000	$10,000	$10,000	$10,000	$10,000
5	$11,040	$12,762	$16,105	$20,113	$24,883
10	$12,189	$16,288	$25,937	$40,455	$61,917
20	$14,859	$26,532	$67,275	$163,665	$383,376
30	$18,113	$43,219	$174,494	$662,117	$2,373,763

The difference in results over long periods of time over just a few percentage points is huge; it is stunning. This is the miracle of compounding. When your investment returns start to earn money, and these returns, too, start to earn—this is putting money to work, and the single most important reason to start investing right away.

A comparison similar to the following often appears in various 401(k) and IRA brochures, but is nevertheless worth repeating. Let's say Alice graduates from high school and reads this book and decides to invest in the stock market. From age 20 to 30, she saves $2,000 per year and invests it. That's less than $170 per month, approximately the cost of an espresso drink per day. After she reaches 30, she stops her contributions and just leaves her balance in the brokerage account.

Her friend Bob, however, does not have Alice's foresight. He spends all of his paychecks in the early years and, by the age 45, realizes that he too has to plan for retirement. He puts away $15,000 per year for 20 years. By the time they are 65, Alice will have $896,000 and Bob will $859,000—despite the fact that she contributed a grand total of $20,000 compared to $300,000 for Bob.

The bottom line is, the earlier you start, the better. Time is on your side.

3 Invest for the Long Term

Over the long term, stocks have outperformed bonds and treasury bills with less risk.

Over the long term, staying out of the stock market is more risky than being fully invested.

This statement is certainly going to cause some controversy. How can I say that? At the time of this writing, in September 2008, the Nasdaq is still below 50% of the level it reached eight years ago, in 2000. We are also in the midst of a credit crisis of historic proportions with a number of venerable financial firms failing practically overnight. It is accompanied by a bear market with all major averages down over 30% from their highs several months ago. If that's not risky, what is?

The key to this claim lies in definition of what exactly constitutes "long term" and how you define "risk." Let's take these concepts one by one.

Since 1900, the stock market returned an average of nearly 10% annually. The traditional competition to stocks, bonds and treasury bills, only returned about 4% during the same period. One dollar, invested in the stock market in 1900, would have grown to over $20,000 today. That same $1 invested into bonds would be worth only $60. Rule 2 states that compound interest is good. Indeed.

The domination of the stock market has been rather consistent over shorter periods as well. As explained in *Stocks for the Long Run* by Jeremy Siegel, over any 5-year period, stocks outperformed other investment types over 70% of the time. For 10-year periods, this number rises to

80%. Over 20 years, it goes to 95%. Finally, over 30-year intervals, stocks have always outperformed other investment types. I would say that this defines the first element in my claim, namely that long-term should mean over 20 years or more.

You may wonder whether a holding period of 20, or even 30, years applies to your situation. After all, chances are that you are not planning to hold a particular stock or a mutual fund that long. However, I am talking about the holding period of the entire portfolio, regardless of the number of changes you may make in it. And this holding period, in most cases, will run for several decades.

Now, let's take a look at risk. Traditionally, many people think of risk as the possibility of losing a substantial part of their investment. Looking again at performance of stocks vs. bonds and treasury bills, over any period of 10 years or longer, the maximum loss suffered by stocks was less than that suffered by bonds and treasury bills. Even in the worst 5-year period, the maximum loss from stocks was only one percentage point higher than that from bonds.

In mathematical terms, risk is often defined as the standard deviation of average annual returns. Standard deviation measures how widely spread the values are from the average. Using this formal definition, again, over any period longer than 20 years, stocks carried less risk than competing investment types.

The superior performance of stocks does come with a price of short-term volatility. Back in the 1800's, Mark Twain said: "October is one of the peculiarly dangerous months to speculate in stocks. The others are July, January, September, April, November, May, March, June, December, August, and February." Over a few months or even years, no one can argue that this danger is all too real. However, history shows that over longer terms, stocks are in fact less risky, if one sees risk as lost opportunity. In the long term, the risk of investing in "safe" securities and realizing subpar returns is far greater than the risk of short-term fluctuations in the stock market.

4 Understand Mutual Funds

It is convenient to invest in mutual funds, but you need to be aware of the fees and underperformance of these investment vehicles.

A mutual fund is essentially a collection of stocks and/or bonds. Most mutual funds are "actively managed," which means that the fund manager makes decisions on what stocks to buy and sell. Index funds, on the other hand, are designed to follow a given market index, such as the S&P 500. Index funds trade stocks when a change occurs in the underlying index, which does not happen often. Thus, they trade very infrequently, and essentially can be automatically managed.

Mutual funds come in a variety of flavors. There are stock funds, bond funds, and balanced funds, which are a combination of the two. Stock funds vary depending on the size of the companies they invest in (small cap, mid cap, or large cap) and investing style, such as growth or value. There are funds dedicated to specific industry sectors, countries, or geographic regions. Altogether, there are several thousand actively-managed funds to choose from.

The simplest way for a beginning investor to start is with a mutual fund. A mutual fund is liquid, meaning that its shares can be bought and sold upon request. It has the advantage of diversification, since you are buying into a basket of different securities simultaneously. And finally, a professional money manager will be taking care of your investment.

Interestingly, the last two advantages can also be thought of as drawbacks. Often, mutual funds are invested in too many companies, or over-diversified. Thus, even a great performance by several of the fund's holdings can have a negligible influence overall, resulting in mediocre returns. And professional money management generally does not result in better performance. In fact, the opposite is often true.

All mutual funds charge fees for their services. After all, they are for-profit companies and that is how they make their living. The most important fee to understand is the fund's expense ratio, which varies, but for many funds is in the 1.5% to 2% range. This means that each year the fund charges you the above percentage of your assets for the privilege of managing your money. While a couple of percentage points doesn't seem like much, over a long period of time it will make a huge difference. Just take a look at the compound interest table in Rule 2.

The expense ratio itself typically consists of the management fee, which covers management salaries, distribution fees for sales and marketing expenses, and various administrative costs, such as book-keeping, etc. In addition, certain mutual funds feature front or back loads, sometimes up to additional 5%, which is deducted from your balance when you invest or withdraw money from the fund. This is a huge, well, load, on the performance.

Predictably, those fees lead to a significant underperformance of mutual funds. Compared to market indices, only 20% of actively managed funds fare better. I was certainly shocked when I learned of this many years ago. Indeed, why pay all those management fees if the managers can't beat the market? And finally, the fees are charged re-gardless of fund performance, and are imposed even if the fund loses value.

Of course, the intent of this discussion is not to urge you to sell all mutual funds you may have. There are actively-managed funds that consistently produce superior returns. But it would be good idea to check on your fund fees and your fund's performance compared to its peers. This information is readily available on a number of financial websites (see Appendix B).

5 Consider an Index Fund

If you are content with market performance and have no time or desire for stock research, index funds are for you.

We saw in Rule 4 that a typical mutual fund frequently underperforms the market, primarily due to the management fees it charges. Many other rules in this book describe various ways you could employ to outperform the market. If, however, you are content with keeping abreast of the overall market performance, then an index fund becomes a very attractive option. And it is not such a poor option—you can expect to earn about 10% annually, which was the average market return for the last 100 years.

Index funds are passively managed. Unlike a typical mutual fund, for which the fund manager selects the fund holdings, index funds follow a predetermined composition of a given index in exactly the same proportion. For example, if one stock represents 0.5% of the S&P 500 index, that same stock will also weigh in at 0.5% of an S&P 500 based index fund. An index funds trades only when a company is removed or added to the underlying index, which does not happen often.

There are several reasons why index funds fare better than mutual funds. First, they have lower costs, because they don't need a full-time fund manager and staff to research and select fund holdings. These are already predetermined by the composition of the index. Second, mutual funds usually have a very high turnover rate (85% is the average—this means that each year, 85% of fund holdings are replaced), which generates high trading costs. Finally, mutual funds have cash reserves that can sometimes be as high as 10% of the fund value. Cash reserves are good during market declines but, long term, stock markets go higher, and cash becomes a drag on the performance. Overall, the fees charged by index funds typically stay below 0.5%. That is at least 1.5% less than fees charged by mutual funds—and the difference goes directly to your pocketbook.

While funds based on the S&P 500 index are the most common, other indices are also used. There are index funds based on the Wilshire 5000 (an index based on the market value of all stocks traded in the U.S, as opposed to 500 companies for the S&P 500), Dow Jones Industrial Average (30 Dow Jones stocks), Russell 2000 (small-cap stocks), S&P Midcap 400, and many others. Different indices can produce quite different short-term results but, long-term, the performance tends to even out.

In recent years, an alternative to index funds has emerged—depositary receipts. S&P depositary receipts, or "spiders," have the same composition as an S&P 500 index, but unlike index funds, they trade during stock exchange business hour, just like shares of a stock. Shares of mutual and index funds, on the other hand, can only be redeemed on a daily basis. Also, depositary receipts don't have to distribute capital gains each year, which lets your investment compound tax-free, and that is a big advantage (see Rule 13). However, as for any stock, you do have to pay brokerage commissions when you trade, and this may be a consideration if you prefer to make deposits at regular intervals (for example, monthly). Finally, similarly to index funds, depositary receipts exist for a variety of indices. The most common are "diamonds," representing the Dow Jones Industrial Average, and "cubes," which are proxies for the Nasdaq 100 index.

Whether you choose a traditional index fund, or depositary receipts, you are virtually guaranteed to achieve market performance and thus beat the majority of actively-managed funds with almost no effort on your part. Some of you may not have the time or the desire to actively research stocks. If that is the case, index funds become very attractive.

6 Hedge Funds: Read the Fine Print

Hedge funds could be suitable for qualified investors, but make sure you read all the fine print.

A hedge fund is a variation of a mutual fund. The basic idea—to pool investors' money together and have it managed by a professional—is the same. Unlike mutual funds, however, hedge funds are not regulated by the Securities and Exchange Commission (SEC), and thus can use a variety of trading strategies and techniques that mutual funds are sometimes not allowed to use. These strategies include selling short, using options, derivatives and arbitrage, investing in anticipation of certain events (such as company buyouts) and even investing in other hedge funds (so-called "funds of funds").

The very word "hedge" implies that hedge funds must employ some kind of hedging technique. That is one of the misconceptions about these investment vehicles—while some funds do hedge against market downturns, many don't. Another misconception is that hedge funds are very volatile. Indeed, some of them are, but many may not use any leverage at all, or may even employ various techniques to reduce volatility.

Similarly to mutual funds, hedge funds typically charge a "maintenance fee" which is usually 1–2% of assets under management. However, in addition to that and unlike mutual funds, hedge funds also charge a "performance fee" which is normally 20% of profits. So why would you consider a fund with even higher expenses?

The justification from the hedge fund industry for this fee structure is that, despite its overall higher cost, it actually aligns shareholder and manager interests better. It is said that the lucrative performance fee attracts talented money managers to hedge funds—after all, unlike for mutual funds, a hedge fund manager's salary is directly proportional to the fund's performance. Also, many hedge fund managers invest their own money into the fund, which creates yet another incentive to deliver good results.

So, does this actually translate into a better deal for you? According to a CXO study, from 1994 to 2006, hedge funds, after all fees, did outperform the market averages by one half of a percentage point. However, since hedge funds are not bound by SEC rules, there is limited information available, and sometimes it is hard to get an accurate picture of their performance. It is very important to understand hedge fund strategy, risk profile, and past performance, if available. This information is usually provided in the fund's Private Placement Memorandum.

Liquidity could be another consideration before investing into hedge funds. While mutual funds trade on a daily basis, liquidity for hedge funds varies greatly. Some managers require lock-in periods of several years before you could withdraw your investment. While this requirement has some merit—it forces you to take a long-term view and could prevent you from selling out at market bottoms, this is definitely something you should be aware of. Even if there is no lock-in period, hedge funds usually allow redemptions only after several months' notice.

The final distinction is that hedge funds are usually available only to so-called "qualified" or "accredited" investors, who are essentially high net worth individuals. According to the SEC definition, a qualified investor has either at least $1,000,000 in net worth, or has an income of at least $200,000 per year if single or a combined income of at least $300,000 per year if married. Also, the minimum investment into a hedge fund starts from $50,000 and ranges to millions of dollars (in contrast, you can invest as little as $100 into most mutual funds).

The bottom line is that you have to proceed with caution. Hedge funds vary greatly in their strategies and risk tolerances, information about them is limited, and there are also considerations of fees and liquidity. But finding a good hedge fund could be very rewarding.

7 You *Can* Beat the Market

There are several important advantages that an amateur has over professional investment managers.

In 2004, there were over 8,000 U.S. mutual funds. Worldwide, there were over 50,000. In addition, there are thousands of hedge funds and various investment newsletters. Scores of financial planners advise their clients on ways of investing their money in an efficient manner. These professionals are very likely to have years of experience in the financial industry, relevant education, as well as a large staff to help them make their decisions. What chance do you have, as an amateur, to succeed in a stock-picking contest on your own?

Amazing as this may sound, the odds are actually stacked in your favor in being able to beat the pros. The reason for that lies in the way Wall Street works.

In Rule 4, we saw that mutual funds, as well as investment advisors, charge fees for their services. That is the primary reason for mutual funds to lag the benchmarks; in fact, over the last 60-year period, an average mutual fund under-performed the indices by about 2% per year. You, doing research on your own, don't have these expenses.

Even if mutual fund fees are taken out of the calculation, an average fund *still* manages to fare worse than the market. Apparently, investing is one field where an MBA or a Ph.D. from a top business school as well as years of experience don't translate to superior job performance. Many fund managers believe that they can outsmart or time the market (see Rule 9 on why this is not a great idea), and therefore tend to be very active traders, churning their entire portfolio in a matter of months. In addition to being a poor strategy, this also incurs high transaction costs that eat into performance.

Several years ago, *The Wall Street Journal* ran a so-called "Dartboard Portfolio." This portfolio was selected by hanging several pages with stock quotes from *The Journal* on a wall and throwing darts at them. Wherever the darts landed, the corresponding stocks were included in the portfolio. The Journal staff then tracked this "Dartboard Portfolio" and compared its performance to that of mutual funds. As you might have guessed, it did fare better than most of its professionally managed competition.

Another reason you have a distinct advantage is your average trade size. In this case, size matters—and the smaller, the better. There are many funds with total market capitalizations of $1 billion or greater. Just because of its size, such a fund usually holds hundreds of positions in its portfolio so that it doesn't end up owning more than a certain percentage of total shares outstanding in a company it invests in. From my experience, it is quite difficult to come up with 30 great investment ideas, so it must be extremely hard to come up with hundreds of them. As a result, such funds end up owning a number of mediocre companies, and even a great performance by one of its holdings is likely to have a negligible effect on the overall portfolio. This is a standard problem of over-diversification. Also, if the manager identifies a good company, it is hard to purchase a stake at the current price—a large fund needs to acquire a significant portion of the company to make it worthwhile, and by this very action, drives the share price higher. A similar situation occurs when a fund tries to sell its position. You, as a small investor, don't have to worry about affecting the market by your trades.

The most important advantage is your own background and experience. You can invest in industries and companies that you already understand. Wall Street analysts, even the ones that specialize in a certain field, usually only have a superficial and a theoretical familiarity with it. Again, your experience and first-hand knowledge matters and puts you on top.

Of course, just because you could beat the market, there are no guarantees that you will. Hopefully the rules presented in this book with arm you with tools and ideas that will help you to achieve this goal.

8 Market Declines Happen

Stock markets declines happened before and will happen in the future. They are a natural part of the market cycle.

Over the long term, stocks outperform other liquid investments such as bonds and treasury bills. That performance does come with a price of volatility and periodic market declines. A decline of 10% to 20% from a peak is called a correction. Corrections are very common in the market and occur, on average, every 18 months or so. A bear market is on that is in a decline of 20% or more. An average bear market results in a loss of about 30% of market value from the peak and lasts 9 to 18 months (sometimes longer).

During the last 100 years, we witnessed 18 bear markets, which included nine protracted bear markets with declines of 30% or more and the greatest of all bear markets, the 1929 Crash, when the stocks dropped almost 90% over 3 years. From the high of 1973, the market dropped 45%. In the crash of 1987, the Dow dropped 23%—in one day! This volatility plays an important part of a traditional definition of what risk is—namely, a possibility of losing a substantial part of your investment in a relatively short period of time.

The causes for market declines vary. Often, stock market drops are associated with economic difficulties. The memories of the Crash of 1929, which was followed by the Great Depression, still linger. However, behaviors of the markets and the economy can also be decoupled from each other. For example, the 1987 crash did not have any effect on expanding the economy and was simply a correction, as some contend, of overextended equity valuations. Another common reason for market declines is some kind of uncertainty—for example, before an armed conflict. Markets would drop on worries about an impending clash, and would rally once the fighting began. That was the case in 1990, before and during the beginning of the first Iraqi war. At present (September 2008), we are experiencing the deepest financial crisis since the Great Depression, caused by a number of factors, including a severe correction in housing market.

Whatever the reason, declines in stocks happen. They are, in fact, recurring and expected events. It may be difficult for you not to be emotionally worried about market swoons—after all, it is not fun watching the value of your savings dwindle in front of your eyes. In rational terms, however, worrying about that is just about as productive as worrying about rainy weather. You don't assume that several days of rain signify the beginning of the next Great Flood. But if you believe financial media during market setbacks, not only will you be convinced that the Great Flood is upon us, but also that the Ark has already sailed and all hope is lost!

I find it very helpful to think of this analogy when the next regularly (or irregularly, as the case may be) scheduled market decline arrives. Granted, it will take time (sometimes several years) for the market to fully recover, but I have full confidence—and historical data to back me up—that it will.

At the time of this writing, we are in the midst of the 19th bear market of the past century. It is also the 10th severe bear market with a drop from the top of over 30%. And without a doubt there will be the 20th bear market and the 11th 30% decline. These pullbacks are all but certain; they are a natural part of the market life cycle, just as winters and summers are natural parts of the life cycle of our planet. A savvy investor should not fear or get upset with such corrections, but be prepared to take advantage of the low prices and a coming upswing in the market.

9 Market Timing Doesn't Work

Buying at the bottom and getting out at the top looks great in hindsight. Unfortunately, it is quite impossible to do this reliably.

The ability to time the market has been the Holy Grail for traders since the days the exchanges were invented. After all, if you look at a chart of any stock or an index and see all the peaks and valleys, it is very natural to wish, "If only I could buy near this bottom and sell at that top..." I have a friend, Rob, who believes that he should be able to do just that and who gets very upset at himself when it doesn't work out. For years, I heard comments from him like, "I was so stupid, I sold this stock and it continued going up!" Or, "I was thinking of selling, but was too busy to call the broker, and it went down! What an idiot I am!" I tried to explain to Rob that what he wanted to achieve was impossible, but I don't think I succeeded. Hopefully, I will have better luck with you.

For the proponents of market timing, hindsight is a very powerful weapon. They believe that various indicators can accurately predict future market movements. There are many such indicators out there, from completely non-financial to extremely technical. Some better-known examples include the Super Bowl indicator (some winning teams are better for the market than others), the hemline indicator (the higher the hemlines on currently fashionable women's skirts, the better for the market), the trading volume, volatility, technical trend indicators, various economic indicators, etc. The proponents of a given indicator would point out that it correctly predicted market movements a certain number of times in a given time period.

The problem with that thinking is that it is backward-looking and, given enough powerful computers, can be manipulated into showing nearly anything. For example, the performance of the S&P 500 index from 1983 to 1993 was almost flawlessly predicted by... the production of butter in Bangladesh! For a while, I had my own indicator—whenever I went on vacation, the market would go up. Believe it or not, it actually was quite accurate for over five years, but it stopped working when the current bear market started in 2007. And I thought I finally had the secret!

While many mutual funds claim that they do not time the market, they nevertheless attempt to do so by increasing or decreasing their cash positions. Others, such as tactical asset allocation funds, admit to having market timing as one of their primary strategies. A number of investment newsletters also assert that they have this skill by advertising their successful past trades.

As far as I know, there is no proven record of success of anyone who tries to time the market. I don't know of any market timers or traders who built a fortune in stocks using this strategy. The investing greats, such as Benjamin Graham, Warren Buffet, Peter Lynch, in contrast, believe in a steady-as-she-goes approach, keep their holdings for years and do not advocate jumping in and out of the market. Of course, you may have heard of stories of someone who sold his entire high tech portfolio in 2000. But more likely than not, this is typically attributed to the law of big numbers or simple luck, rather than skill in calling a market top.

A very clear corollary to this rule follows. Read on...

10 Stay Invested at All Times

Jumping in and out of the market jeopardizes your returns. Stay the course instead.

If you accept that it is impossible to time the market on a consistent basis, as discussed in Rule 9, then logically it follows that you should always stay invested in the market. This conclusion is certain to raise some controversy. The power of hindsight is just too great, and you do hear stories of other investors who had the foresight of not only avoiding bear markets, but also of hedging or even going short during the slide.

You can spend a lot of time looking at the charts that show past performance but today, now, no one can say for sure which direction the market will turn tomorrow. Various studies have shown that past movements cannot reliably predict future results. In one test, eight charts were given to a number of traders who used technical analysis. Four of them were charts of actual stock performance, and the other four were randomly generated by a computer. The traders were not able to distinguish between the real and simulated charts.

Staying out of the market, you are also likely to miss some big up days. If you invested $10,000 in 1997, it would have grown to $22,000 by 2006. Missing ten best days during that time would have reduced the return to $14,000. Missing 20 best days would reduce it further to $9,600—below your original investment. Granted, it could take some talent to specifically miss the best days, but nevertheless I think that this illustrates the point.

Staying fully invested doesn't mean that you have to keep holding the stocks that you already have. In fact, it is necessary to keep re-evaluating your portfolio and make sure you are holding the best selections you can possibly choose (see Rule 25). In any kind of market, one can always find stocks with good current prospects.

What about hedging? Hedging is essentially an insurance against market declines. Note: many, but not all, hedge funds practice hedging; see Rule 6.

One of the most common hedging techniques is a purchase of put options, for example, on a market index such as the S&P 500. Hedging, however, could be quite expensive and, used constantly, may cost you many percentage points in decreased overall performance. While hedging could prevent you from suffering big losses during market declines, its constant high expense in the long term, during flat or rising markets, could drive your overall returns significantly lower—very possibly lower than if you did not have any hedging to begin with.

I started my investing career in 1987, after the big correction that year, and stayed fully invested ever since. Yes, I do admit that this was true even in 2000. Moreover, I had very high exposure to tech stocks, since I have a technical background and was actively involved in that industry then. I did have the foresight, however, of not buying into dot com enterprises with no revenues. But, as you know, even solid tech stocks with real earnings fared very poorly during that bear market. In late 2000 and 2001, I re-evaluated my portfolio and sold many tech stocks and replaced them with other equities, while staying fully invested. My portfolio originally suffered together with the rest of the market, but fully recovered to its year 2000 highs in about four years. Granted, it would have been nice to sell out at the top in 2000, but according to many analysts, markets were already overpriced back in 1995. Remember "irrational exuberance?" Should you have sold then?

Today, in September 2008, as in 2000, we are in bear market territory. The market may continue to go down, but it may also turn up tomorrow. No one knows for sure. I do believe that it is prudent to stay the course rather than tempt fate by jumping in and out.

11 Keep Records of Your Performance

You should know how your portfolio is performing so that you can compare it to market indices and other benchmarks.

I would often have a conversation like this with a prospective client. "So," they would ask, "How is your fund is doing?" I would tell them. To which a very common comment is something like: "Well, I bought 200 shares of XYZ and it doubled in five months!" Or, alternatively, they would tell me a horror story about another stock they had, which crashed and burned. Then, I would ask what the performance of their overall portfolio was. Very few people can answer than question accurately and quite a few have no idea how to define or calculate it.

Every portfolio has its share of winners and losers. But knowing only how each of your individual holdings performs is similar to not seeing the forest for the trees. You need to know how your overall portfolio (or a portion of it that you may be actively managing) fares in relation to comparable market indices. Based on this track record that you build over the years, you can make informed decisions for the future. For example, if you consistently outperform the S&P 500, that's great. If not, then it might be a good idea to buy an index fund instead or hand over money management to someone with a good track record.

So, how does one calculate overall performance? In the simplest scenario, when you don't make any deposits or withdrawals during a year, it is the difference, in percentage terms, of the total portfolio value at the end of the year and the beginning of the year.

It is important to make sure to take into account all your liquid investments: stocks, mutual funds, 401(k) and IRA funds, as well as cash that you may have in your accounts. Cash is very important in this calculation—it is a drag on performance in rising markets and a cushion in declining ones.

In real life, cash flows in and out of our brokerage accounts frequently, for example via deposits to your 401(k) plan with every paycheck. In this case, it is not enough to just add all withdrawals and subtract all deposits made during the year to calculate the difference between values at the end and the beginning of the year. The timing of these withdrawals and deposits becomes very important.

To illustrate this concept, consider the following two hypothetical portfolios. Portfolio A was worth $100K on January 1 and additional $100K was deposited on January 2. On December 31, it was worth $220K. Portfolio B also started with $100K, also received a deposit of $100K, but on December 30, and also finished the year at $220K. Despite exactly the same ending and starting values and the deposit amounts, the return of Portfolio A was just over 10%, while the return of Portfolio B was almost 20% (in the first case, $20K grew based on $200K, and in the second, only on $100K).

	Portfolio value, in thousands				
	Jan 1	Jan 2	Dec 30	Dec 31	Return
Portfolio A	$100	$200	$220	$220	10%
Portfolio B	$100	$100	$120	$220	20%

As you can see, the exact calculation of total return is not trivial. It involves tracking each dollar invested for short intervals (i.e. daily) and integrating those into the total. Many brokerage firms do provide their clients with the return of their account. In addition, financial software packages such as Intuit Quicken or Microsoft Money can calculate accurate returns for all of your accounts. These packages also keep records of your past performance so that you can see how you fared, for example, in declining or raising markets.

It is very important to know your overall performance, in order to know where you stand compared to other investment vehicles available in the marketplace. What was your return over the last year? Last three years? How about last five years? This knowledge will help you to make educated decisions for the future.

12 Set Realistic Expectations

Set portfolio return goals that can be actually achieved on a consistent basis.

I recently saw the following aphorism: "I invest only in vodka. That is the only thing that guarantees 40%." That, of course, refers to the percentage content of alcohol in vodka. But, amazingly enough, there are quite a few people (typically with little or no investment experience) who believe that consistent 40–50% returns in the stock market are achievable. Certainly, it is easy to be influenced by certain unprincipled financial publishers that advertise "157% profit" on one of their trades. Of course, that trade was most certainly cherry-picked, and the return annualized—that way, a 10% gain in a month translates into a triple-digit annualized return. The guy in the office bragging about his outsize returns can also add to the expectation of consistently high results. Most likely, however, that same guy is not talking about the dogs in his portfolio that he is likely to have. Also, he probably doesn't even know what his overall return is (see Rule 11).

At 50% growth, $10,000 will increase more than 3,000-fold to over $30 million in twenty years. In ten more years, you will be a billionaire—and you don't even need to start a new Microsoft for that! It is true that in one of those years, you could well make 50%—in fact, that was the return of the Nasdaq index as recently as 2003. The year before, however, it declined by over 30%. The broader S&P 500 index gained 38% in 1995 and lost 22% in 2002. Single-year extremes are to be expected, but it is not realistic to expect them to repeat themselves year over year.

The historic average market return over the last 100 years is 10%. The key word is "average"—I don't believe that the market returned exactly 10% in any recent year. The last decade of the previous century was quite remarkable in terms of stock market performance; the average annual return during that period was 18%. Even experienced investors believed in the popular theory of the "new economy" and expected to achieve 20% yearly returns indefinitely. These hopes were dashed in the bear market that started in 2000.

In any event, you can easily duplicate the market by investing in an index fund. This obviously has the advantage that you don't have to spend any extra effort researching individual stocks. Assuming, however, that you do aim to outdo market averages, and that 50% and even 20% is not realistic, what is? Aiming for 12% per year, or 2% more than market average, is a worthy goal. Anything more than 15% per year would be spectacular. These returns should be computed according to the guidelines in Rule 11, with all commissions, other expenses, as well as cash accounted for.

Some of my perspective clients are somewhat underwhelmed when I tell them about these goals. I do believe, however, that it is important to set goals that are achievable and realistic. If you expect to make, for example, 25% year after year, you are quite likely to get frustrated for not being able to achieve this objective. You will feel obliged to change your investment strategy or take unnecessary risks, and those are usually roads to failure.

13 Minimize Your Expenses

Improve your net returns by cutting down on your largest costs—taxes and commissions.

One of the ways any business can increase its profits is by minimizing its expenses. Think of investing as running a business. Most likely, you operate from the comfort of your home, and thus you don't have typical business costs, such as rent, utilities, etc. You do need to spend certain amounts on accounting, market publications, subscriptions and other tools, but your biggest expenses are likely to be taxes and commission costs.

Many investors don't think of taxes as an expense, and concentrate on their pre-tax returns. Instead, you should focus on the overall after-tax results of your investment activities, and that result is likely to be very different. Consider the following example: Let's say investor A starts with $10,000 and keeps these funds fully invested in the market, with no trading for 20 years, realizing 15% pre-tax annualized return. At the end of this term, after paying 15% long-term capital gains tax, he is left with $139,115. Investor B also starts with $10,000 and also has the same rate of return, but he trades each year and therefore has to pay short-term capital gains taxes at 28% each year. After 20 years, he is left with $77,767, a little more than half of what investor A gets to keep. Due to their trading patterns and current tax laws, A's effective (post-tax) rate of return is 14.1% and B's rate is only 10.8%, while their pre-tax returns are the same. That is why master investors prefer to hold "forever." This is yet another argument in favor of long-term investing.

One tax-related strategy that most investors are well aware of is year-end selling of losers in order to reap capital losses to offset capital gains. This is quite useful; however, be aware of the current tax laws—specifically, the $3,000 capital loss limit per year and the wash rule that does not allow you to purchase the same security within 30 days of its sale, if you wish to claim a capital loss.

Taxes are very important. However, you should never let tax considerations overrule your overall investment strategy. If you have an appreciated stock that, according to your evaluation, needs to be sold, then sell it—even if you have to pay a considerable amount in capital gains taxes. You are at the risk of losing much more if you don't sell and the stock turns lower. It is OK to pay taxes—after all, if you pay a lot in taxes, you made much more for yourself.

Finally, commission costs represent another significant source of your expenses, especially if you trade often. For example, let's say you trade 100 times per year at $10 per trade for a total yearly cost of $1,000. If you start with a $10,000 portfolio, the trading costs represent 10% of the principal and will absolutely kill your overall returns. Even if you start with $100,000, that extra 1% drag on performance will cost you over $112,000 after 20 years (assuming 10% annual return on your investment). Find a broker with lower commission costs, or, even better, reduce the number of trades. Be aware that compound interest (Rule 2) will turn pennies into dollars over the years and find ways to minimize your costs.

14 Control Your Emotions

Don't do anything related to investing due to an emotional response. Be rational.

For many people, investing can be very emotional. After all, you are placing your hard-earned money at the whim of the market, over which you have no control. When the market declines, or experiences severe corrections (and it does that regularly, see Rule 8), and you see your holdings drop in value, there is always an urge to do something about it. In declining markets, fear takes over and the natural instinct is to sell to prevent further losses.

The opposite of fear is greed. In an advancing market, greed takes over and produces a desire to buy more in order to reap greater profit. That is a very natural and typical reaction. After a 1000-point drop in the Dow, people are pessimistic and want to sell, not buy. After a 1000-point advance, sellers are few and far between and optimism abounds. As a fund manager, I am certainly aware of this phenomenon. I typically receive new contributions during the times of market advances, which, short-term at least, often are precisely the wrong times to invest.

These decisions are based on the desires of your heart, not your brain. They are driven by emotion and not by reason, and the resulting choice is often incorrect. Does this mean that when market goes down, we should buy more, and when it advances, sell? Of course not. In all cases, we should use all tools available to us to evaluate the current situation and make a rational decision based on available data, and not because a market pundit on TV declares that the sky is falling.

The emotional response can be evoked not only because of overall trends, but also because of specific news about a company that you invest in. We all know that share prices can sometimes move violently in response to certain news about the company. An emotional reaction to this situation would be a desire to do something, anything, to "fix this problem." This is a very dangerous state of mind that often produces the worst investment decisions. Our job as investors is to calmly analyze the situation and make a rational choice based on the available information. This analysis could lead to a decision to sell, buy more shares, or, more often than not, do nothing at all (see Rule 32). Impulse buys and sells are the worst things you could do, that will inevitably lead to regrets later.

Let me tell you a story about the Magellan Fund. From 1977 to 1990, the Magellan Fund was managed by Peter Lynch, and during this time achieved extraordinary average annual returns of nearly 30% per year. Many consider Peter Lynch to be the best mutual fund manager ever. Nevertheless, the majority of people who invested in the Magellan Fund during Lynch's tenure actually lost money. How is that possible? While achieving excellent returns, Magellan Fund was certainly subject to overall market fluctuations and had its share of ups and downs. Apparently, many investors made emotional decisions to put the cash in during the good times and take it out during the bad.

In popular TV science fiction series "Star Trek," Mr. Spock is the science officer on the starship "Enterprise." Mr. Spock is from planet Vulcan, whose inhabitants live by relying on reason and logic, without any interference from emotion. I don't recall that subject of investing comes up in "Star Trek," but Vulcans should be very good at it. Try to think like Mr. Spock when it comes to your portfolio. And, as the Vulcans say, live long and prosper!

15 Be Patient

Short term, there is often no correlation between a company's fundamentals and its stock price. Long-term, there is 100% correlation.

Being emotional can be hazardous to your investment returns. Being patient has the opposite and positive effect.

A few times, I had the following discussions with prospective clients. They were considering investing in my fund, but, since they didn't know me well, they wanted to "test the waters" by starting with a small amount. The idea then was to see how my fund performed for the next couple of quarters, and, if everything went well, they would go ahead with the total sum they planned to invest.

While this cautious approach certainly seems reasonable, it actually doesn't work if the "testing period" is measured in quarters. Over that interval, my returns as a manager could be good or poor, they could beat or underperform the overall market, but they would be meaningless. They will be random. They will depend on luck, and not on skill. The testing period is too short.

So what should be the length of the interval to compare returns? It depends on how certain you want to be. Let's say that you are a very good stock picker and your expected long-term return is 5% above market average (and that is no small feat). Due to market fluctuations and various unexpected factors, the probability of your underperforming the market over one year is over 30%. That's one chance in three—and it is due essentially to bad luck. Over two years, that probability drops to 25%, which is still quite significant. Over five years, it goes down to 15%, and over 20 years to less than 2%. That is why the testing period of a couple of quarters makes no sense; the shortest one should probably be at least 2–3 years.

This statistic also demonstrates that it is very hard to identify good or poor money managers. There is no question that there are talented and skilled managers in the industry. Magellan Fund delivered extraordinary returns for 13 years. However, just looking at the two, five, or even ten-year returns may not be sufficient. There is always a chance that these returns were achieved due to luck rather than skill.

What does all this have to do with patience? Short term, performance of any stock is influenced by overall market conditions, perceptions of the company in the marketplace, company news and many other factors. Very often, stocks and fundamentals can move in opposite directions. A patient investor knows that if the price of the stock goes up, it doesn't necessarily mean that he is right, and conversely, if it goes down, it doesn't mean that he is wrong. It will take time to figure that out. The point is, short term, stock performance is random. Long term, however, this performance is 100% correlated to company earnings. Over time, stock fundamentals will inevitably win over the short-term randomness and therefore patience is one of the most important factors in successful investing.

16 Keep It Simple

You should be able to explain your investing thesis to a 12-year-old in three sentences.

Occam's Razor is a principle attributed to the 14th century English philosopher William of Ockham. The basic idea is that a theory that makes the least amount of assumptions while explaining a certain phenomenon is often the correct one. Translated from Latin, Occam's Razor says "entities must not be multiplied beyond necessity." In modern language, this principle is often stated as "All things being equal, the simplest solution is the best." And informally, it is sometimes referred to as the KISS principle—"Keep It Simple Stupid."

Occam's Razor is often quoted in relation to various scientific theories in areas of physics, computer science, etc. It has some applications to criminology, where the simplest explanation of a crime tends to be the correct one. I also believe that it applies to stock selection. Suppose you are evaluating a number of stocks to invest in. You should have a justification of why you are considering buying each one of these stocks. The one with the simplest explanation would probably be the best investment. In other words, keep it simple.

While this may seem, well, simplistic, it makes sense. Applying this rule would steer you towards investing in easily-understood companies as opposed to ones operating in complex industries or having many moving parts. It is quite easy to understand how a business like, for example, McDonalds or Nike operates as opposed to a complex biotech or high-technology company.

That, by the way, is the reason Warren Buffet never invested in high tech companies (and was criticized for that in the 1990's)—he did not have as clear understanding in his mind of the exact ways these companies make money.

I am not saying that you should sell all of your high tech holdings and reinvest them into Coca-Cola. If, for example, you worked in the industry and/or have a good relevant background, you may have very simple and clear reasons in your head why a certain company could be successful, while another might not.

In general, however, I do have (again) a very simple guideline. You should be able to explain to a twelve-year-old why you intend to invest into a certain company, preferably in no more than two or three sentences. That is very important. Look at the stocks that you own. Why do you own them? Playing devil's advocate, how easily can you convince yourself that these particular stocks will do well?

In his book *Beating the Street*, Peter Lynch writes about a portfolio management experiment at St. Agnes middle school in Arlington, MA. The students learned basic principles of Wall Street and were provided with some financial publications. Then, with $100,000 of play money, they created their own portfolios that competed with each other. While this experiment had to be necessarily short to fit into one semester, the selections were tracked over a two-year period. In that particular experiment, an average portfolio outperformed the S&P 500 index—a feat very few fund managers can accomplish.

Clearly, these children did not have access to the wealth of fundamental and technical financial information that professionals use to analyze investments. Their selections were essentially made based on common sense. While common sense and simplicity alone are not sufficient, they nevertheless should play an important role in portfolio selection.

17 Buy What You Know

Invest in the companies that you understand.

The phrase "Buy What You Know" was introduced by Peter Lynch in his classic book *One Up on Wall Street*. This rule was one of his most important, if not the most important, investing principles. It should be yours, too. Simply put, it means you should use your familiarity with a product or an industry as your advantage in choosing a stock to buy.

We have already talked about the significance of having simple reasons for investing in a company. Now, in addition to that, you should have good understanding of how this company operates. If you do, then you probably have a good handle on various risks associated with investing in this company. And your success as an investor depends on your ability to ascertain the risks.

There are several aspects to understanding a business. Here are some questions that you should be able to answer if you are considering investing in a company. First, how does it make money? For example, for most retailers, the answer to that is quite obvious. Other companies may not sell directly to end customers and could have very complex sales channels instead. You should have a very clear picture of how their revenue generation works. Who are your company's customers?

Second, do you know the company's competitors and partners? The success of any company will depend on the actions of its competition, as well as its partners and suppliers, so you should have some familiarity with those stakeholders, too.

Third, what risks and what opportunities do you see for this company in the future? Are there any possible events that would affect the company's business one way or the other? What are the worst case and the best case scenarios?

It is not too difficult to understand a retail or a fast food company. Companies in other industries could be a lot more difficult to analyze. I know that this is very true in high tech, where innovation happens rapidly and the competitive landscape changes on a daily basis. That is where your own experience and background comes in. Use your intimate knowledge of a process, product, company, or a whole industry to identify potential winners that you know about.

They say the grass is always greener on the other side. This adage applies to investing as well. Sometimes, a doctor would invest in a small technology startup, not knowing what the difference is between a hard disk and internal memory. Conversely, an engineer might buy a biotech stock with an uncertain new drug pipeline, without understanding the FDA approval process. And all that is done in the name of diversification. It is all good, but not if you diversify a portion of your portfolio to zero.

Now, diversification is indeed important in maintaining a balanced portfolio (see Rule 22). In fact, if your field of expertise happens to be narrow, investing only in what you know well could prove to be a very risky strategy and overexpose you to one particular industry sector. There is actually a train of thought in the investment community that advocates avoiding buying what you know, for that specific reason.

As an investor, try to find the middle ground in this argument. You should definitely use your expertise and experience to help you make your stock selections. At the same time, continue doing research and educating yourself in other areas of the market. It is not too difficult to be able to understand how a company works by answering some basic questions discussed above, without necessarily becoming an expert in the related field.

18 | Buy Businesses, Not Stocks

When you buy a stock, consider yourself a partial owner of a real business, not of a piece of paper.

While many successful and well-known investors follow this rule, it is most often attributed to Warren Buffett. He said that if stock market were to close tomorrow and stay closed for five or ten years, you should still be comfortable holding your investments. Can you say that for all stocks in your portfolio?

Buying a business is an investment, while stock trading is not. When you place a buy order with your broker, you are about to become a part owner of the company involved. Granted, your share is likely to be very small, but you should always think that you are purchasing a fraction of a business, with all the rights and obligations that such ownership requires. This is very different compared to speculators' view—they are likely to treat their purchases as pieces of paper that can be traded back and forth with no regard to the underlying security.

While this distinction may at the first glance seem artificial, it is nevertheless very important. Thinking as a prospective part owner of the business is very helpful in evaluating it based on its fundamental economic factors, rather than by a recent stock chart. Do you really want to own a piece of, say, Home Depot or Starbucks? If you do, then company sales and earnings, its products and markets, competition, and management will be of great importance to you. On the other hand, current charts, share price trends, investor sentiment toward this stock and various technical indicators should not affect your judgment. In other words, putting yourself into the proper state of mind when making an investment decision will help you to make sure this decision is sound.

The following analogy applies. When you are shopping for a new car, chances are that you are not thinking of exchanging it in a few months for another one. You will keep it for at least several years. You take your time to read automotive reviews, talk to dealers, do a test drive, consult with your friends, etc. You do your homework. Apply the same thought processes and level of thorough research to the business that you are considering investing in. It is quite amazing that there are many people who take months investigating various refrigerator models and shopping for a good deal, and yet they have no problem putting down 20 times more cash for a stock they just spent 10 minutes reading about on the internet.

The movements of stock prices and stock market in general have no impact on the business (with an exception of an IPO, when the company receives cash proceeds). Good companies will continue to make profits and grow, and their shares will rise. This will happen regardless of short-term stock market fluctuations. Own a piece of such a company and you will be well rewarded in the future.

19 Boring Could Be Exciting

Dull businesses in low growth industries not followed by analysts can often produce superior investment returns.

Everyone likes excitement in their lives. Applied to investing, excitement is often associated with owning a hot stock in a high-growth industry. However, it is the unappealing, even boring, businesses in low-growth fields that usually bring consistently high returns.

There are multiple reasons for this. First, if a stock is "hot," it necessarily implies that it is very popular and therefore well known by fund managers, financial analysts, and individual investors. Its business prospects have been evaluated multiple times, various analyst reports have been written, and the stock price reflects them. Quite often, that stock price could also reflect rather strange reasons why the investment community likes the company. For example, during the internet boom, share prices of many companies rose sharply simply because these companies changed their name to include "i," "e," or ".com." In any event, since everyone knows about this company, you are not likely to discover something new about it that would give you a unique advantage. You are better off moving away from the herd (see Rule 20) to greener pastures.

Second, hot companies usually operate in complex businesses, such as biotech or high-tech. After all, it is a lot easier to get excited about a company that promises a new wonder drug than an outfit that produces a laundry detergent. However, running a complex business is necessarily complicated and often invites scores of competitors, particularly in high growth sectors. For example, when in the 1980's or 1990's a technology company came out with a new chip design, dozens of competitors employing very bright people tried to reverse engineer that chip, to figure out how to make one that was better and a faster. And it was usually available on the market within a few months. So each company in this field has to stay on top of its business, or be out of business altogether. It is not easy. That is why there are not too many chip companies left today.

By contrast, this level of cut-throat competition is not found in not-so-exciting industries like toothpaste production or junk storage. The rate of change is much slower in traditional sectors than it is in biotech or high tech. There are simply fewer companies that are interested in operating in these areas. It is easier to run them too. Peter Lynch said that if a business looks like any idiot could run it, sooner or later any idiot will be running it. The giants of today, like Wal-Mart or Coca-Cola, started as small and rather boring businesses of general merchandise and soft drinks. Yes, we all know about Microsoft too, but for each Microsoft there were countless companies in software manufacturing that did not survive. The odds of picking a winner in a boring industry are much better.

Finally, just as it is hard for management to run a complex business, it is hard for you as an investor to understand and analyze it, unless you happen to have a strong background in that area (see Rule 17). Dull and boring businesses are a lot easier to evaluate. Nevertheless, few analysts bother to follow these companies, and therefore they tend to fly under the radar of the investment community. They have little institutional ownership and thus a large percentage is often owned by insiders. These factors are all positives. Obscure companies in unsexy industries, followed by few, if any, analysts, and with high insider ownership do not automatically guarantee a winner, but it is a great starting point for further research.

20 Be Different

Following a currently fashionable investment strategy is not a recipe for success. Stay away from the herd.

The term "herd behavior" refers to actions of individuals in a group without planned direction. Herd behavior in animals is a result of natural evolution, to increase their chances of survival. For example, by keeping as close as possible to the center of a large herd, buffalos can better avoid a predator attack, while at the same time protecting their young.

Herd behavior applies to humans too. When you see two restaurants, one almost empty, and the other full of people, you immediately assume that the second restaurant is better. This is a typical example—you make your decision based not on the information available to you (such as restaurant reviews, for example), but on choice made by other people.

There are two primary reasons for herd behavior. First, it is hard to assume that a very large group of people can be wrong. They may know something that you don't. And second, there is pressure to conform. Most people don't want to be mavericks and risk not be socially accepted as a result. Although in our restaurant example, the group may well be correct in deciding that the full restaurant is better than the empty one, herd behavior applied to investing usually ends with devastating results.

The primary examples of herd behavior in investing are bubbles and crashes that inevitably follow them. The first recorded bubble in history is the tulip mania in Holland in 1637. At its peak, one tulip bulb fetched an equivalent of 20 years' earnings of a craftsman, or 12 acres of land! The South Sea bubble that devastated the English stock market in 1720 showed that even the brightest individuals are susceptible to herd mentality. Sir Isaac Newton lost a considerable sum of money in the market crash that subsequently followed. There are more examples throughout history, including the famous crash of 1929, the recent internet bubble of 2000 and the ongoing collapse of the housing market that peaked in 2005. I recently saw a bumper sticker on a car that said: "Oh God, please! One more bubble!" The next bubble will certainly happen, but as always, it will only be recognized as such after its peak.

Today, the stock market is often driven by herds of financial institutions and management companies. If there is a strategy (such as buying internet stocks in 2000) that is popular at the moment, it is very tempting for fund managers to employ that strategy as well, so that their clients don't feel left out. If it works out, they will be happy. If not, at least the manager is not alone in making this mistake. Thus, since so many people employ it, this strategy could well become a self-fulfilling prophecy and may work well for some time. After all, if everyone is buying tulip bulbs, their prices will rise.

And watching these prices rise, it could be very tempting for you to join the herd as well. However, history has shown that this is hardly a winning investment strategy. An investment thesis is rarely proven correct just by the number of people who believe in it. In investing, the herd is usually wrong. Always do your own homework and research. Don't be afraid of being different, and look where others don't.

21 Select Companies of the Right Size

Companies in the middle of the market capitalization range present best growth opportunities without excessive risk.

All publicly-traded companies are categorized based on their size, or market capitalization. Market capitalization is the amount the company is currently worth, and it is calculated by multiplying share price by the number of shares outstanding. There are four typical categories with the following approximate ranges of market cap (exact definitions may differ between various brokerage houses):

Micro-cap stocks	Below $200 million
Small-cap stocks	$200 million to $2 billion
Mid-cap stocks	$2 billion to $10 billion
Large-cap stocks	Above $10 billion

When you consider adding a stock to your portfolio, you should be well aware of its market cap. The risk/reward profiles can vary greatly. Intuitively, it is clear that the smaller the company size, the riskier is the investment. The flip side is, of course, that the potential rewards can be huge as well.

Compared to other categories, investing in large-cap stocks (and especially in super-large-cap, those with market cap of $100 billion or more) usually presents less risk. After all, chances are that Coca-Cola or Intel will still be around for the foreseeable future. Nevertheless, there were certain periods when large-cap stocks suffered tremendous declines—some

Nifty Fifty stocks in 1970's and large technology stocks in 2000 dropped over 70%, while a number financial companies went bankrupt in the current financial meltdown of 2008.

Large-cap stocks also represent big areas of the markets and many of them are internally diversified. This means that you can get away with owning just a few of them and this reduces the amount of work required to follow your holdings. On the other hand, it is difficult for large companies to grow and become even larger. It is much harder to increase earnings 20% annually for a $100 billion mega-corporation than for a $500 million entity. Many large-cap companies become victims of their own success in terms of revenue and earnings growth. For example, Microsoft used to grow strongly before 2000, when it reached $400 billion market cap. Then, the growth finally slowed and the stock stagnated ever since as a result.

Mid-cap stocks represent the breadth of the market. Many of these stocks are on their way from small-cap to large-cap status and therefore can still grow rapidly while having lower business risks compared to small-cap equities.

Small-cap stocks and the upper echelon of micro-caps probably present the best opportunities in the market in terms of potential appreciation. Indeed, from 1925 to 2006, small-cap stocks outperformed the S&P 500 by nearly two percentage points. After reading Rule 2, you know this is a huge difference. Despite this, many people resist in investing in small-caps because of the perceived high risk associated with them. Investing in small-caps also involves researching more stocks and taking a dedicated effort in following them. Nevertheless, without a doubt, these are the stocks that can experience the fastest earnings and therefore share price growth.

And finally, you must have heard of "penny stocks" and "pink sheets." They represent the lowest priced and rather infamous subset of microcap stocks—those that trade below one dollar per share and/or are listed in the over-the-counter market. These stocks are very illiquid and can be easily manipulated—we have all received junk emails about the next great thing priced only at $0.75. Most importantly, there is lack of reliable and publicly-available information about these companies. You are well advised to steer clear of them.

It is of course up to you to decide what ranges of market cap you are comfortable with. In my own portfolio, I prefer to buy stocks with market caps between $200 million and $20 billion. This certainly provides a very wide selection of equities to choose from while avoiding high risks from micro-cap stocks and uninspired growth from super-large-caps.

22 Know How Many Stocks to Own

Make sure you have the bandwidth to follow all the stocks in your portfolio.

All of us hear about the virtues of diversification almost on daily basis, through financial newspapers, magazines, and television. Diversification is a risk management technique that, applied to stock market investing, requires spreading your total investment among multiple companies. Your holdings should also be diversified between different industries and even different countries or geographic regions.

There is good reason to do this. If all your holdings are concentrated in a couple of securities, bad news about these companies can send your total portfolio value plunging. Even if you have a number of different companies but only in one industry, overall trends in that industry can expose you to a high amount of risk.

I know of several people who were not very interested in investing, but, being employed in the high-tech industry, had the usual perks associated with their jobs. They participated in stock purchase plans and owned stock options, and their employer matched their 401(k) contributions in company stock. Not only a considerable part of their assets depended on the company performance, their job depended on that too! Now they know of the risks of over-exposure to one company: in the bear market of 2000, stocks of high tech companies crashed and many went out of business.

One way to achieve instant diversification is to buy an index fund. In the example of the S&P 500 index fund, you are buying into each of 500 companies that comprise that particular index. That way, you are also guaranteed that your returns will be better than of most actively-managed mutual funds (see Rule 5). If, however, your goal is to achieve superior market returns, then you have to select individual securities for your portfolio. The immediate question then is: how many different stocks should you own in order to be properly diversified?

In Rule 23, we will show that owning just ten stocks eliminates most of the risk of investing in one company. Also, we will see that if you already own 20 stocks, adding more equities has almost no effect on that risk. That doesn't mean, however, that you should always limit your portfolio size to 20. There is really no right answer to the question of how many stocks you should own. It all depends on the characteristics of these companies, as well as on how much time you can afford to spend researching companies.

The market capitalization of your companies matters. If you invest in huge conglomerates, such as GE or Exxon, they are already internally diversified and you can get away with holding just a few of them. On the other hand, small-cap and especially micro-cap companies (valued under $250 million) are more volatile and it is a good idea to hold more of them (I recommend 20 to 50) to smooth out the risk. At the extreme (that you are probably not involved with), venture capital funds invest in hundreds of privately-held startups, knowing that the vast majority of them will fail, but hoping that a next Microsoft or Google will more than compensate for these losses. At that stage, it is a numbers game.

Your ability to follow these companies plays a vital role. I do not advocate "buy and forget" investing; you should constantly keep tabs on your holdings and react to changes in their businesses (see Rule 25). Peter Lynch used to own 1400 stocks at Magellan Fund, but he did have a staff that helped him to be up-to-date on these companies. I suspect that you don't have that staff, and so do you, alone, have the bandwidth to do that research for 30 stocks? How about 50? 100? If not, consider reducing the number of your holdings.

Rule

23 | Beware of Over-diversification

Having too many stocks in your portfolio does not help to reduce the risk and could lead to neglecting your holdings.

Diversification is important. It is an essential tool in reducing the risk of your portfolio. However, you should use it with restraint, and abusing it can prove to be too much of a good thing.

Let us address diversification from a scientific point of view. Since it is a risk management technique, and risk is often mathematically modeled as standard deviation of investment returns, we need to discuss that last term. Standard deviation is a measure of variation of a given set of values from their expected average. For the S&P 500, the standard deviation (computed annually) over the last 100 years is around 19% and the average annual return is 10%. This means, that in any given year, there is about a 2 out of 3 chance that the S&P return will be in the range of its average plus or minus one standard deviation, or between -9% and 29%.

Now, let's look at a portfolio consisting of just a few random stocks. In any event, the expected average return will still be 10%. The standard deviation will vary, however (the following calculations are presented in Joel Greenblatt's book *You Can Be a Stock Market Genius*). If there are only two stocks in the portfolio, the standard deviation is 37% and so your expected range widens to an interval from -27% to 47%. For 6 stocks, the standard deviation drops to 26% and the range narrows to -16% to 36%. For 10 stocks, the range is from -13% to 33% and for 20 stocks it narrows to -11% to 31%.

These results are quite interesting. Note that investing in just 10–20 stocks, statistically speaking, is not much different from investing in the overall index, because the expected range of returns is quite similar. That is why the returns of the Dow Jones Industrial Average, which consists of only 30 stocks, are so similar to those of the S&P 500 (500 stocks) and of the broadest index Wilshire 5000, which tracks 5000 stocks. The range of returns is also very wide, which means that owning hundreds of stocks in your portfolio does not in any way guarantee the stability of the investment.

There are two widespread misconceptions about diversification. First, you don't need to own dozens or hundreds of companies to be properly diversified. Second, the law of diminishing returns definitely applies here—adding more stocks to the existing portfolio, if it already has more than 20 stocks, has a negligible effect on its diversification.

Another issue to be aware of is that diversification only helps to avoid so-called "non-market risk," that is, risk associated with specific companies in your portfolio. The "market risk," on the other hand, refers to the risk of investing in the whole market and it remains the same even if you hold 5000 stocks in your portfolio.

The lesson from all of that is that, for many of you, investing in 20 stocks should provide adequate diversification. Adding more holdings presents several issues. First, it is going to be more and more difficult to come up with great ideas in terms of selecting a company with out-standing business prospects. Second, it will be harder and more time consuming to follow all of your holdings. And third, even a big move by one of your companies will have a small effect on the overall portfolio.

These are the standard problems of many mutual funds that have to invest in hundreds of companies due to their size (see Rule 7). These problems are well known in the industry; in fact, over-diversification is often referred to as "deworsification." Fortunately, you don't have to follow mutual fund rules and can avoid deworsifying your portfolio.

24 Know When to Sell

Sell when you find a better place for your money.

As an investor, you probably know that a decision to buy a stock is much easier than a decision to sell. Once you own a stock, you somehow feel psychologically attached to it, and in order to sell, you need a good reason—a much better reason than prompted you to buy it in the first place! The current stock price usually doesn't help to make this decision. If it is higher than what you originally paid, then you think that the stock might go higher still. If it is lower, you'd like to get back to your purchase price so that you could at least "break even."

I am certainly guilty of thinking along both of these lines. In the late 1980's, I owned a number of high tech company stocks: Oracle, Sun Microsystems, and Intel among them. I sold all of them for what I thought was a respectable profit, only to see them rise more than ten-fold in subsequent years. On the other hand, I held on too long to Krispy Kreme Donuts, only getting out of it when it lost more than two-thirds of its value. I am sure that you have similar experiences.

According to the well-known investor and author Philip Fisher, if you did a good job in selecting a stock in the first place, "the time to sell it is—almost never." Warren Buffett agrees. Nevertheless, we all make mistakes and therefore we need a strategy as to when to pull the trigger and sell. A basic rule of thumb is to revisit your reasons for purchasing the stock in the first place. (Hopefully, you didn't buy it because your cousin Bob said it was hot. In this case, sell now!)

Are these reasons still in place? Has something changed in the company's business or its competitive situation? Will you buy this stock again, at its current price? If not, then consider selling.

Probably the most important reason for selling is that you identified another opportunity that presents a better place for your money. Your original investment thesis may still be intact, and you may expect the stock to go up, say, 15% per year. But if you think you found another that has the potential to increase by 25%—that could be a valid reason to sell.

Keeping your portfolio balanced may present yet another reason for selling or at least reducing your position. Let's say you were fortunate enough to pick a big winner so that it now represents a significant part of your portfolio. Should you sell? There is no good answer to this one—it depends on your own tolerance of risk. Experience says, "let the winners run," which inevitably leads to these equities taking dominant positions in the portfolio, and of course this increases the risk of volatility. I am not too happy about this right now, as two of my largest holdings dropped more than 50% from the top in this current bear market, but I still believe in their long-term potential. I also remind myself that Warren Buffett at some point had about a third of his total assets in Coca-Cola. But in any case, it is up to you to decide whether you can stomach this kind of volatility.

Other grounds for selling include poor financial performance, untrustworthy management, increasing competition—but all of these could really be inferred from the very first rule of revisiting your original rationale for purchasing the stock. That, together will identifying better investment opportunities, are the primary reasons to sell.

Note that current company valuation, or its stock price, usually should not figure in this determination. The price could be double what you paid for it, or it could be half. The market has no memory and doesn't know what you paid. The past doesn't matter, only the future does—and so you need to re-evaluate the company from the present forward. Don't attempt setting price-related goals ("I'll sell when I make 50%" or "I'll sell when I break even"), as they are based on the past. Other poor reasons for selling include basing your decision on overall market or economic conditions (see Rule 27), as well as on commonly-used stock valuation metrics (such as the P/E ratio). Growth stocks often appear overvalued based on these metrics.

25 Re-evaluate Your Portfolio

Perform a check-up of your portfolio on a regular basis.

In the science fiction TV series "Star Trek," the Borg consists of cybernetically-enhanced humanoid drones arranged into a closely-knit collective with a hive mind. The primary strength of the Borg is a superior ability to adapt to any external threats, such as enemy weapons. While one or two drones may die, the rest of the collective adjusts and that particular weapon becomes ineffective. In the series, the Borg becomes one of the major threats to humanity.

In real life, too, everything that is successful needs constant adaptation to changes in the surrounding environment. Plant and animal species continuously evolve to increase their chances of survival. Once-dominant dinosaurs could not adapt in time to the rapid change of climate caused by a meteor striking our planet. We all know what happened to them.

If you don't want your portfolio to share the fate of the dinosaurs, it needs to adapt to the constant changes that take place in the competitive situation of each of the companies that comprise your portfolio. Generally, I believe in a "buy and hold" philosophy—it takes time for an investing thesis to fully play out. And quite often it takes years. But this philosophy should not be confused with "buy and forget" investing, where you purchase a stock and don't bother to check on it for long periods of time. I know of some people who actually actively embrace this philosophy. "I bought this stock," they would say, "and

I want to see what it does for me in ten years." This also happens quite often with the retirement accounts from the companies you no longer work for—these accounts tend to be neglected frequently.

You might get lucky: selecting a Microsoft or a Wal-Mart in its early stages would indeed do wonders for you in ten years. But that's not a good reason to stay uninformed—keeping tabs on Microsoft during its growth years would still bring you that profit. At the same time, it might have helped you to avoid huge losses on, for example, some of the dot com companies in the early 2000's. CMGI went from $1300 per share (adjusted for reverse stock split) to $3 in two years. It trades about $12 at the time of this writing—and that's much better than hundreds of internet companies that went out of business.

Select a certain time interval and check on your stocks at least once during that time. A monthly or a quarterly portfolio evaluation is reasonable. You could even do it only once per year, but I would not recommend it doing less frequently than that.

How do you perform this evaluation? It is quite straightforward. Look at each of your holdings and apply Rule 24 to see if it is time to sell it. Has something changed in your original investment thesis? Would you buy this stock again, at its current price? Do you have a better place for your money? Has it grown so much that it represents too much of your portfolio? If indeed you decide it is time to sell, you should have a replacement ready. So, it is a good idea to also have a so-called "watch portfolio"—a group of equities that you also follow, perhaps not so closely as your actual holdings, but from which you can select a new candidate to buy. But note that it doesn't have to be a brand new stock—sometimes, the best stock to buy is one you already own.

We all know that stock prices can move violently when earnings are announced. It is a common occurrence, when a company announces earnings of 24 cents per share instead of the expected 25 cents, the price could drop by 20% or more. If there are no fundamental changes, price movement alone is hardly a reason to sell. The same is true when the price is dragged down with the overall market decline. However, changes in the competitive environment can be more significant. In 2006, the U.S. Congress passed a law prohibiting internet gambling. That wasn't good news for internet gambling software provider Cryptologic. While one could decide to hold it, waiting for the company to redeploy its offerings to European and Asian markets, such an event did merit selling the stock.

26 Don't Listen to Market Pundits and Analysts

In the media, you can always find some to agree with and also to disagree with. But no one can predict events.

I heard about the following scheme to establish yourself as a market expert who can always predict whether the market (or an index, or a particular stock) will move up or down within a certain time interval, for example, one week. Let's say you send your weekly newsletter to 1,024 thousand subscribers. In the first week, you send a letter to 512 thousand readers predicting that the market will go up, and another letter to the remaining 512 thousand with a prediction of a down movement. Then you wait until the week is over and see what the market actually did. If it went up, you continue working with the first half of your subscribers, and if it went down, with the second. Again, you send two newsletters predicting up and down movement, now to 256 thousand readers each. After the second week is up, you continue working with the group that received correct predictions only.

You can see where this is going. At the end of the 10th week, you will have one thousand subscribers that received correct predictions from you for 10 weeks in a row! Indeed, you must be a guru, and these people will be privileged to let you manage their money.

This is a rather simple illustration of the law of big numbers. That streak of 10 correct predictions in a row came from making 1,024 separate binary guesses (meaning they had two outcomes only—up or down, similar to a coin flip).

The modern financial services industry makes far more complicated guesses on a daily basis. In magazines, newspapers, internet, TV, and other media, all kinds of experts give their opinion not only on general market direction, but on various economic conditions and indicators for the United States and other countries. They comment on individual stocks, currency exchange rates, bonds, etc. And these opinions are not binary—many are predicting certain stocks or indices to move a certain amount within a certain period of time. If you tune in to CNBC, Bloomberg, or other financial channels, these opinions are given around the clock, on a 24/7 basis. Very often, highly qualified commentators present completely contrasting forecasts.

Similarly to our simple newsletter scheme, the law of big numbers applies here as well, this time in a real-world situation. The number of forecasts and predictions is so high that some of them are bound to come true. Here are a few examples.

I recall that, in 1987, at least two market commentators correctly predicted the market crash that occurred later that year. They became celebrities within the industry and appeared on a number of TV shows, gave numerous interviews, etc. Yet, both were unable to repeat their successful predictions on anything else that mattered. It is quite clear by now, that calling the 1987 crash was a stroke of luck, not skill.

Here's another example. In 2006, a certain hedge fund manager correctly called the coming mortgage meltdown and earned billions of dollars by shorting mortgage-backed securities. Was this also a stroke of luck, or was that skill? The jury is still out on that one.

The point is that it is quite unproductive to listen to various market commentators and analysts. The number and range of opinions given is so vast that you can invariably find views similar to your own, as well as views that are exactly the opposite. More often that not, a prediction comes true because of the law of big numbers, rather than the skill and foresight of the analyst.

Commentators and analysts are paid to present their views on future market events. That, after all, is their job. As investors, however, it is our job to do our own research and form our own opinions.

27 Concentrate on Your Stocks

The market as a whole should not be relevant to you. Concentrate on your stocks instead.

Economic and market analysis and commentaries, presented by various sorts of media, generally are not useful. This also applies to the stock market itself; constantly monitoring various market averages is not good use of your time. Nor does it help you to achieve better returns. In other words, the stock market should not be relevant to you, a long-term investor.

There is a saying on Wall Street that "a rising tide lifts all boats." While all investors prefer rising markets, there is no guarantee that your particular stock is moving the same way. A stock index is computed as a certain average of equities that comprise that index; your stock may not even be a part of the index, or, if it is, it could be moving in the opposite direction. Clearly, it is not the market that makes individual stocks move—it is the other way around. If you are in college and the average grade in your class is better today than the year before, that doesn't mean that your grade is better, too. Your grade depends only on you, and not on other students. This is quite obvious, but somehow many investors expect the "market" to influence their stocks.

Of course, stock prices are affected by a variety of factors, including the general state of the economy, investor sentiment, etc. But since predicting these conditions is just as unfeasible as timing the market itself (see Rule 9), don't spend time worrying about issues that you cannot control. Your time will be much better served by keeping up-to-date with the companies in your portfolio, as well as continuing to do research and finding new opportunities for investment.

Even if you guess the overall direction of the market correctly, the only reliable way of benefitting from it would be to buy (or sell) an index fund. If you are correct about the trends of a specific industry (which, in my opinion, is just as difficult as market timing), you could profit from a related sector fund. But that, of course, does not in any way guarantee that all stocks in this industry will move in the same direction. Even in the greatest bull and bear markets, there always were (and will be) numerous examples of companies bucking the overall trend. During the tech boom of the 1990's, Digital Equipment Corporation failed to see the move towards personal computers and was eventually acquired by Compaq. On the other hand, graphics card manufacturer Nvidia prospered during the subsequent tech implosion in early 2000's.

It is much better to keep buying great companies than trying to guess what the market will do next. Don't consider selling your holdings just because you think that the market is headed lower. Conversely, don't buy in anticipation of a higher market ahead. It doesn't matter whether the Dow is at 10,000 or 14,000. That is not important. What is important is that you are monitoring your current or prospective holdings and are up-to-date to whatever is happening with these companies. You can always find great companies in any kind of market. Over time, your investing thesis, if correct, will undoubtedly prevail over general market trends. Concentrate on your stocks, and don't worry too much about the market. It will take care of itself.

Concentrating on your stocks, however, doesn't mean that you have to check prices several times a day. That is exactly what my ex-coworker, Dan, used to do with the balance of his 401(k) plan. He just graduated from college, and so his total holdings were still very small. Nevertheless, Dan called the mutual fund company at least once a day and reported the results to everyone within an earshot. "Today is a good day, I am up $10!" he would say. Or, "Oh, no, I lost $7 since yesterday! There goes my lunch!" While Dan was very wise is opening his 401(k) early, clearly, checking with the fund company that often is not productive and is very distracting.

28 Recognize and Learn from Your Mistakes

Recognize that you are not invincible. Analyze and learn from the mistakes that you will inevitably make.

A successful investor is well aware that he is not always right. Once his mistake becomes evident, he takes corrective action immediately. Contrast that to a typical investor who often hangs on to a losing position hoping that he will eventually break even. His pride is preventing him from admitting he made a mistake. Pride, like other emotions (see Rule 14), is very hazardous to your investment returns.

Not a single investor on this planet has always been correct. Rule 29 states that you don't need to be always right, and that your winners will overcome your losers. But, it would certainly be nice if you had fewer losers to begin with, and if your losses were smaller. The first step to achieve these goals is to hone your ability to recognize that you made a mistake. You had your reasons to buy a stock, and something went wrong. The competitive situation changed, the management turned out to be dishonest, the demand for company product suddenly dropped, etc. Once this becomes apparent, liquidate your position and move on. Don't let your pride stand in the way. One of the most successful investors, George Soros, said that ability to recognize mistakes early was the secret to his success.

The second, equally important, step is to use your mistakes as learning experiences. Similar to other things in life, this is crucial to getting better at whatever you are doing and avoiding mistakes in the future. In order to learn how to ride a bicycle, you had to endure many painful falls, but they were absolutely necessary to the learning process. In investing, too, once you liquidate an offending position, you should analyze what exactly went wrong and why. By not repeating the same mistake, you will improve your performance. And often, making fewer mistakes makes a big difference.

Consider the following analogy. Think of investing as a game of tennis you are playing against the market. In tennis, like in many other games, you can win in two ways. First, you can hit winners—strong shots that your opponent can't return. And second, you can cut down on unforced errors—the losing strokes you make that were not forced on you by your rival. Very often in professional tennis, and almost always at my amateur level, the game is won not by the player who hits the most winners, but by the player who makes the lower number of unforced errors.

In investing, your winners are obviously your well-performing holdings. When the market throws its "winner" at you (such as unexpected poor economic news, for example), there is not much you can do. You can, however, avoid making unforced errors on your side and greatly improve your odds of beating the market. Recognizing and learning how to avoid mistakes from your previous games is essential for compiling a good track record.

29 Your Winners Will Overcome Your Losers

The most you can lose on a stock is what you paid for it. But your potential gains are unlimited.

We all make mistakes in life. Investing is no different; in fact, it would certainly seem that this area is very fertile ground for poor judgment. You could well be under the impression that you made more mistakes in investing than in all other aspects of life combined. That feeling is substantiated by the fact that investment mistakes are so clearly obvious after you made your decision. You see that stock going down and you count your losses—there you go, baaad mistake!

The human brain is wired in such a way that it reacts significantly more strongly to the possibility of losing money than to the prospect of a gain. Even though it may have happened years ago, most of us are likely to remember a stock that lost three-quarters of its value, and we still keep wondering how on earth we could have made such a poor decision. But take solace in the fact that you are most definitely not alone. Even the greatest investors made and will continue to make their share of mistakes. It is just not possible to be always right. But the good news is that you don't have to be. Even if only one half of your picks are winners, that could well be enough to compile a great performance record. Furthermore, chances are that you may do well even with fewer winners than losers.

The reason for that is simple mathematics. Suppose your portfolio consists of two stocks that were each worth $10 per share when you bought them. Let's say one of them quadruples, while another is now worth only a quarter of its original value. Contrary to what many expect, your portfolio is far from breakeven. Your winner is now worth $40, the loser is at $2.50, and so your portfolio gained $22.50, or 112.5%!

That is the way the markets work if you keep investing for the long term. The most you can lose on any given stock is only what you have invested in it. On the other hand, your potential upside is unlimited. One investment in Wal-Mart when it was still getting started easily outweighs scores of poor or mediocre selections. That is the principle that venture capital funds embrace. They invest into hundreds of privately-held startups, knowing that the vast majority of them will fail, but one Microsoft or Google will more than compensate for these losses. Of course, this is a very extreme situation—make sure that you have not one, but several solid selections that are capable of carrying your portfolio in the future. Hopefully, the Rules presented in this book will help you in making these choices.

"Let Your Winners Run." There is truth in this old Wall Street saying. Search and keep your winners once you find them. That search is certain to produce many false candidates—it is a natural part of the investing process. Don't get hard on yourself for making mistakes, and expect that you will continue making them. If you follow Rule 25 and re-evaluate your portfolio regularly, your losers should not inflict heavy damage. Your winners will prevail and take good care of your overall portfolio.

30 Insider Buying Is Good

There are many reasons for insiders to sell, but only one reason to buy—they think the price is going to rise.

An insider is an officer of a company or anyone else who has access to confidential information about company operations. According to the SEC, company officers, directors, or anyone with a stake of 10% or more in a company is an insider.

Insider trading information is freely available on many financial websites. In addition, there are many sites devoted exclusively to insider transactions, such as J3 Information Services Group (http://www.j3sg.com/).

In general, you can expect insiders to be selling shares overall. Company executives regularly receive bonuses in the form of stock options; in fact, for many, especially in the high-tech industry, stock-based compensation is the primary source of income. There are many reasons executives may decide to sell: to finance purchase of a new home or a car, for their children's education, etc. Since they typically have a lot of their fortune tied to the company stock, diversification is also a valid reason to sell. However, they have only one reason to buy—they think that the share price is undervalued and is going to rise. And, since these people occupy top positions in the company, they have a far better view than anybody else about what is really going on with the company's business. So when they vote with their pocketbooks, you should listen.

In the middle of 2004, after a disappointing product launch and subsequent loss of market share, graphics card maker Nvidia lost two-thirds of its value in about four months. Company executives knew that it was a temporary setback and bought shares en masse. They were joined by members of the Board of Directors. And indeed, the company introduced new, successful products later that year and improved its financial position greatly. Three years later, Nvidia's share price multiplied tenfold from its lows.

When browsing through a list of recent insider buys, it is important to check if the purchase is significant as opposed to being a token gesture. For example, if a CEO with an annual salary of $500,000 buys $10,000 worth of stock, it does not mean much. If, however, he spends $1,000,000, it is a different story. Also, look for filings where not one, but several insiders buy at about the same time. It helps to know that many executives feel strongly about the company prospects.

Just as with anything else in the stock market, insider buying is certainly not a "sure thing." After all, company managers are people too, and people make mistakes. There are numerous instances of a stock going down even after insider purchases. But, more often than not, insiders know what they are doing.

The ultimate insider is the company itself, and, if a company is buying back its shares, you could also think of it as insider buy. A company has many options of what to do with cash—pay dividends, develop new products, make acquisitions, etc. If it prefers to use this cash to buy its shares at the open market, then it essentially broadcasts its belief that the best place to invest is in itself. That's a very powerful signal worth watching for. In addition, when the company buys back shares and thus removes them from circulation, the earnings per remaining shares rise, which in turn helps the share price to rise as well.

31 Learn to Value Stocks

You have to know what a fair price for a stock is.

Estimating how much a share is worth is the most important decision in evaluating a prospective investment. There is a wealth of available resources, including numerous books and websites that discuss stock valuation in detail. Here are the most common and useful metrics.

The most common valuation method is based on company earnings. The famous and most often used P/E ratio (also known as the multiple) is calculated by dividing the share price by the earnings per share, usually for the preceding 12 months (thus it is often clarified as the trailing multiple). In theory, the smaller the ratio, the more attractive the stock. But of course, it is never as simple as that.

The caveats are numerous. First, P/E ratios tend to be different for different industries. For example, ratios for technology companies tend to be higher than those for utilities. So you should always compare a stock against its peer group, not against the market as a whole. Second, the stock market is always forward-looking (see Rule 33). Often, stocks have low P/E for a good reason, such as poor future prospects; conversely, stocks with a high P/E may anticipate better business conditions. For that reason the common trailing P/E is not as important as the forward multiple, or one-year estimate of future earnings. Third, growing companies deserve higher multiples, since future growth makes a company more valuable. Thus, a new metric, price to earnings growth, or PEG, is often used.

It is calculated by dividing P/E ratio by the earnings growth rate. Generally, if PEG is below 1, the company is considered to be attractively valued. And again, forward PEG is more useful than its trailing counterpart.

What happens if company had no earnings or lost money during a certain interval? This certainly occurs often and in this case the earnings-based valuation tools are no longer applicable. Then, price to sales (P/S) ratio is used, which is calculated by dividing the total market capitalization of the company by its revenue. (If there is no revenue, you are well advised to steer clear!) Again, P/S ratios are different for different industries, and the forward-looking ratio is more important than the trailing one. Price to sales ratio is often used for emerging companies that have negligible or no earnings, or for companies in cyclical industries during the down cycles (for example, airlines or auto manufacturers).

While cash flow is rarely reported on typical financial websites, it is nevertheless often used by investment bankers for valuation purposes. Cash flow is also known as EBITDA, which stands for Earnings Before Interest, Taxes, Depreciation, and Amortization. This measure is useful, because, unlike the P/E ratio, it focuses only on operating profits and therefore could paint a more accurate picture of company financial health.

Another commonly used metric is based on shareholder equity. You can think of it as net worth of the company—it includes hard assets, such as real estate and equipment, cash and other liquid assets. Book value per share is obtained by dividing shareholder equity by the number of shares outstanding. Commonly used price-to-book ratio is then calculated by dividing share price by book value per share. If the result is less than 1, it means that, if liquidated, the proceeds should be higher than the current market valuation. Be careful, however: often the stated hard assets are overvalued by accountants.

These are the most frequently used valuation techniques. It is very important to have a good grip on what they mean and how to use them. They will be indispensable when you try to estimate a fair price for a company stock.

32 Sometimes, It Is OK to Do Nothing

Judge your performance by results, not by the amount of activity.

If you showed up at work and didn't do much except for surfing the web, or if you decided not to go to work at all, chances are that fairly soon you won't have a job anymore. You are paid to perform what your job requires you to do, and if you fail to do that, your employer has to find a replacement for you. This applies to professional money managers as well—they are expected to perform their tasks, whatever they may be, on a daily basis. Unfortunately, in investing, that is not a correct approach.

Contrary to what you may think, a typical investment professional is not paid for making you money. Just like you, he is paid for coming to work every day and doing his job. Market commentators are paid to voice their opinions, even if no one solicited them, and they do this daily on television, on the internet, and in newspapers. Analysts are paid to write their reports, and they do, even though there could be no one who is interested. Investment newsletters have to come up with one or several recommendations per month, and they do, even though that particular month they may have had no good stocks to recommend. And finally, fund managers are paid to invest your money, and so they trade, even though the best course of action could be to stay put. Somehow, investing gets equated to trading.

Realize that in investing, unlike in some other occupations, you are rewarded by results, not by activity. Very often, you may not be able to find a compelling company to invest in, or to come up with good reasons to sell one that you already own. In this case, leave your portfolio alone and do nothing. Chances are, you will find a great investment candidate, and sooner than you may think.

You may be concerned that "doing nothing" means losing a grip on your holdings. But you are only doing nothing in terms of trading—your investment activities should encompass much more than interacting with your broker. Use that spare time to search for other opportunities in the market or to educate yourself about other industries. This will be time well spent.

The desire to "do something" manifests itself frequently during market declines. You see your nest egg dwindle in front of your eyes, and the need to do some action to stop it could be overpowering. If you follow through on that desire, however, you are likely to make a big mistake, as you are letting your emotions take precedence over rational thinking (see Rule 14). Conversely, if the market is moving up very quickly, you may feel the need to catch up, even though by that time the valuations reach unreasonable levels.

In late 1990's, Warren Buffett saw the market as overvalued and refrained from making additional investments even though he had cash available. He was criticized at that time for missing the internet boom, not understanding the "new economy," and underperforming the market. History, however, proved him to be ultimately right, and his inaction prevented his shareholders from suffering the fate of the overall market in 2000. Judge yourself by being right, not by being active.

33 Look to the Future, Not to the Past

Past price history of a stock has no relevance on its future prospects.

"Past performance is not a guarantee of future results." This ubiquitous legal disclaimer can be found in every mutual fund prospectus. It is not given by your broker when you trade; nevertheless, it is warning that you should heed whenever you buy or sell a share of a stock.

The stock market as a whole does not reflect the past or even the present. Instead, you can think of it as a forecasting mechanism that attempts to predict economic conditions in the future. An interesting illustration of this is market behavior around recessions. During recessions, economic activity drops, and so do company earnings. It would be natural to expect the markets to decline during these periods of reduced economic levels (a recession is formally defined as a period of two or more consecutive quarters of GDP decline). But that is not the case.

According to a Bloomberg study of nine recessions that occurred from the 1950's until today, the S&P 500 actually showed an average gain of 1.2% from the beginning to the end of a recession. But the market performance was significantly worse before recessions started. An average maximum drop from market peak to market trough during the period from six months before the start of a recession through the end of the recession was 23.4%. And an average maximum gain from recession start through six months after recession end was 42.4%. This shows that markets anticipate recessions and start to decline well before a recession actually begins. During a recession itself, markets anticipate recovery and usually commence their ascent well before a recession runs its course. The same forward-looking mechanism applies to individual stocks too. When a company reports earnings, the reaction in stock price is very often driven not by actual results reported and how they compare to expectations, but by forward guidance of expected results for the next quarter or the remainder of the year (if provided by management). There are numerous examples of stocks tanking after an excellent earnings report because the following quarter was not going to be as great. That is one of the reasons why common valuation metrics, such as P/E or P/S ratios should be considered with a grain of salt. They are based on the most recent 12-month period and therefore are backward-looking. For example, stocks with low P/E ratios are not necessarily bargains if their future earnings are expected to decline.

This could seem quite straightforward and intuitive, but past price history of a stock often influences our investment decisions. It is very natural to look at a chart, see that a stock was trading at $100 one year ago, and decide that the current price of $45 is a good deal. If you happen to hold that stock, you may be tempted to keep holding it at least until it returns to its previous high levels. After all, if it traded at $100 before, most likely it will trade at that level again. Well, maybe it will and maybe it won't. But the fact that it did so one year ago is of no significance whatsoever. The Nasdaq market as a whole is still ways off its high of 5,000 reached in March 2000. The past is gone; only the future matters. Evaluate prospects of a stock based only on current information available. I would rephrase that mutual fund disclaimer to read: "Past performance is irrelevant to future results."

34 Use, but Don't Abuse, Margin

Understand margin requirements clearly, and don't borrow more than 15–20% of the portfolio value.

If you open a brokerage account, you can typically select whether you'd like it to be a cash or a margin account. In a cash account, you can purchase stocks only with the cash available in the account. Certain types of IRA accounts are cash only. The majority of the accounts can be opened with margin, however.

Margin is a loan that you obtain from your broker to purchase a security if you don't have enough available cash in your account to pay for it. This loan, like all other loans, carries interest, and is secured by other holdings in your account. The interest rate usually changes with the prime interest rate, and decreases slightly as the amount you borrow increases. Under the current laws, the amount you can borrow may not exceed 50% of the total value of your other marginable securities. Note that each brokerage house may have slightly different rules on what constitutes a marginable security. For example, stocks under $5 often are not eligible for margin. Certain other stocks could be deemed by your broker to be very volatile, and the amount you could borrow could drop to, say, 30%.

Margin is a leverage tool. Let's say you have $100,000 in your account. Under the 50% rule, you can borrow another $100,000 and buy, for example, 2000 shares of a stock at $100 per share. Your loan, $100,000 is now 50% of the total value of the account, which is $200,000. If the stock goes up to $125 per share, your account is now worth $250,000. If you sell at this point and return $100,000 to the broker, you are left with nearly $150,000 (after margin interest), an almost 50% gain compared to 25% rise in the stock itself.

As you may imagine, however, leverage works both ways. If that stock drops to $75, then your account is now worth $150,000, a 50% loss in investment after repaying the margin loan. At this point, your account equity is $50,000, or 50% of the loan amount. If that percentage were to drop further, you may get an infamous "margin call." The margin call is issued if the ratio of account equity to loan amount drops below a predetermined amount. It depends on the broker, but typically this threshold is 30%.

In our example, if your stock drops further to $65, you will get the margin call. This means that you will have to deposit more cash or other securities in the account to make sure that the equity-to-loan ratio stays above 30%. If you don't have these additional funds, the brokerage will liquidate your holdings to protect their loan. Sometimes this is not possible—for example, if your company announces a horrific earnings report and the price drops to $40 overnight, not only will you be completely wiped out, you will end up owing $20,000 to the brokerage as well.

In the 1920s, margin requirements were only 10%, as opposed to 50% today. Without a doubt, this contributed to the Great Crash in 1929, and left many investors wiped out and owing additional funds to brokerages that they couldn't repay. This is also what happened to the Duke brothers in the movie "Trading Places" (of course, they were trading orange juice futures that have much less stringent margin requirements compared to stocks).

It is up to you to decide whether the risk of investing on margin outweighs its benefits. Used with understanding and caution, margin could be a useful tool for experienced investors. I don't think that you should ever borrow more than 15–20% of your total portfolio value. Then, the power of leverage could be used to your advantage.

35

Avoid Betting on Options

Most options contracts expire worthless. Exercise caution.

When you open a brokerage account, in addition to choosing a cash or margin account, you can also request option trading privileges. A stock option is a right (but not the obligation) to buy or sell an underlying stock at a specified price within a predetermined period of time, before the option expiration. There are two basic forms of options—calls, which give the right to buy, and puts, which give the right to sell.

A number of books and much information on the internet are available to describe the technical details of option pricing as well as numerous strategies that are possible to implement with stock options. Here are three main strategies that options are used for. First, you could generate high rates of return. Second, you could use options as insurance to protect a stock or your whole portfolio against a decline. And third, you could generate extra income from your existing holdings. The first two strategies require buying options, while the last one involves selling them (see Rule 36).

For now, consider reasons for purchasing options. Options are leverage tools, and unlike margin, the amount of leverage is practically unlimited. Therefore, you could potentially realize a very high rate of return on your investment in an option. Certainly, you saw a number of stock option newsletters that tout their trades that made 876% return in one month. And these returns are indeed possible, but as you may suspect, are highly unlikely. A long-term stock investor only needs to be right about one thing—the overall direction of the stock price. You know that this is not at all trivial—all of us have had our share of losers. An option trader needs to be right not only about the stock price direction, but about the dollar amount of its move, and the time when this move will take place. It is very difficult to be right about all of these factors. You could be correct about the stock potential, but could still lose all of your investment if your stock makes its move after the expiration date. In fact, nearly 80% of options expire worthless.

Another very common strategy is to use options as a portfolio insurance against market declines. It is also briefly discussed in Rule 9. It is now believed that the crash of 1987 was caused, at least in part, by automated portfolio insurance programs. That is rather ironic, because these programs were designed to avoid the tremendous loss of principal that apparently they themselves precipitated. Nevertheless, many investors believe in insurance and keep buying put options to protect their holdings. The price of this insurance, however, is very expensive and you could well end up spending more in option premiums than you would have lost in a market drop if it ever happened.

Since there is always an expiration date involved, which is typically only a few weeks or a few months away, you could think of option buying as market timing taken to the next level. Not only are the odds stacked heavily against you, maintenance of options positions requires daily and sometimes even hourly attention. I am sure you have better things to do in life than looking at charts and worrying about trend patterns all day. Warren Buffett said that stock options and futures should be outlawed. Until they are, exercise caution.

36 Consider Selling Options for Extra Income

You can generate extra income from your existing holdings—but be aware of all the implications.

There are always two sides to every transaction on Wall Street—the buying party and the selling party. This applies to options as well. Now, if most option contracts expire worthless, making option buying a very risky proposition, then option selling could bring you a somewhat dependable income. That is generally the case, but as always, there are caveats to be aware of.

The covered call strategy involves selling (or writing) a call option contract while at the same time holding the equivalent number of shares in the underlying stock. Ideally, the strike price will be higher than the stock price at the time when contract is sold, making the option "out of the money." Then, if the stock price does not exceed the strike price at the time of exercise, the option simply expires. If, however, the stock goes higher than the strike price, the option will be "assigned" and you will be forced to sell your stock at the strike price—which could be lower than the current market price. In any event, you pocket the premium you received for selling the option, giving you that extra income from holding the stock you already have.

The strategy of selling covered calls is often thought of as a conservative approach to stock ownership, as it decreases your risk and provides limited downside protection. The ideal scenario for you is low market volatility, which increases the likelihood of the options expiring out of the money and allows you keep the stock and to continue writing the options. As you know, however, markets do occasionally make large moves, and if that happens, you will not be able to participate fully in the upside. For example, suppose you sell calls for $1.50 per share on a stock that was trading at $48 with strike price of $50. If it advances to $60, you will be forced to sell at $50—and wish you never wrote the calls in the first place. In other words, you still have the risk of not enjoying the potential upside.

You can sell a call option contract even if you don't have a position in the underlying stock. This is sometimes referred to as a "naked call." Naked calls are very dangerous—if the price of the stock advances rapidly, you are responsible for the difference between stock price at expiration and the strike price. Theoretically, your losses could be un-limited. You are well advised to steer clear of selling naked call options.

Another cash-generating strategy is to sell put options. Suppose you are considering purchasing a certain stock, which currently trades at $52 per share, but you don't want to pay more than $50 per share. Rather than setting a limit order at $50 and hoping that the stock drops to that price, you can sell a put option with the strike price at $50. As in covered calls, you always keep the premium you received from the option sale. Then, if the stock stays above $50 at expiration, your option expires, and you created some income out of "nothing" (well, not really; see below). If it drops below $50, your option will be assigned and you will be forced to buy the stock at $50.

As in covered calls, low volatility is beneficial to you as well—you can keep collecting premiums from option sales. In this strategy, there are two major risks coming from large stock moves from either down or up. If the stock drops, you are forced to buy it at the strike price, which could be higher than the market price at the moment. For that reason, put option writers should always have enough cash in case the contract is assigned (and thus the option income really doesn't come from "nothing"). And you also have the risk of not participating in stock up-side—yes, you can generate some cash from option sales, but the stock could make its big move without you.

Generating extra income from your investments is certainly nice. However, as always, there is no free lunch, and that extra income comes with the risk of not being able to participate fully in market advances. Managing option positions also requires a significant time commitment. It is up to you to decide whether these strategies are ben-eficial to you in your particular situation.

37 LEAP-Frog Your Returns

If you can manage the risk, in the money LEAPS can be rewarding.

In Rule 35, I advocated against purchasing option contracts. The primary reason for that is because most options have expiration dates that are, at most, just a few months away. You know that any stock performance over such a short interval is primarily governed by random factors, and thus buying options is more like gambling and less like investing. There is, however, one notable exception.

LEAPS stand for Long-Term Equity AnticiPation Securities, and they are essentially regular option contracts, but with expiration dates from over a year to as far as two years and eight months in the future, usually on the third Friday of January. While two years may still be insufficient for a correct investment thesis to fully play out, it nevertheless has a much better chance of doing so in that time frame compared to the several months you get with regular options. For this reason, LEAPS are definitely worth the consideration.

Note: than LEAPS are not available for every stock that has options traded on it. Many small-caps stocks don't have them. Usually, mid- and large-cap stocks that are actively traded will have LEAPS available. Financial websites, such as Yahoo! Finance lists all offered options for each stock.

You can sell covered calls and puts with LEAPS just as you would with regular options, but I don't recommend it. Many things can happen during the relatively long lifetime of a LEAPS contract, and it stands to reason not to forgo potential gains for the option premium. On the other hand, purchasing call contracts can be quite lucrative.

Consider a real-life example. At the time of this writing, Garmin (GRMN) is trading at about $36 per share. A 2010 in the money LEAPS with strike price of $30 is available for $12 per share. In order for you to break even, GRMN needs to rise to $42 at expiration (at expiration date, there is no time value left in the option, and so its price is simply the difference between the current market price and the strike price), or about 16% from the today's price, which is a very reasonable expectation. After that, each $12 advance in the stock will bring you 100% return on your investment. You are essentially controlling $36 stock with only $12—a 3:1 leverage. Of course, if the stock fails to reach $42, you will lose money, and, if it drops below $30 at expiration, all of your investment will be lost.

Alternatively, you may consider out of the money LEAPS with strike of $50, available for $5 per share. In this case, just to break even, the stock needs to climb to $55, over 50% advance. Then, each $5 rise in the stock will result in 100% investment return. You get more leverage, but the risks are much greater as well. Note that if the stock simply stays at its current price of $36, then all of your investment is lost. In the previous example, you will suffer 50% loss, also a poor outcome, but not as disastrous.

These examples show that in the money LEAPS calls provide enough leverage while carrying less risk than out of the money calls. Nevertheless, LEAPS, being option instruments, are considerably more risky than equities, and there is a real possibility of a total loss. For that reason, limit your exposure to LEAPS to no more than 5–10% of your overall portfolio. And if you are correct, the potential returns can be very rewarding.

38 Don't Rely on Technical Analysis

Technical analysis relies on study of patterns in the past to predict the future. Leave it to the chartists.

Look up a chart of a stock on one of many financial websites, and most likely you will also have an ability to plot a wide variety of technical indicators superimposed on the chart. Yahoo! lists the following: simple and exponential moving averages, Bollinger Bands, Money Flow Index, MACD, Parabolic SAR, Rate of Change, Relative Strength Index, Slow and Fast Stochastic, and Volume. There are many others. These terms could make anybody's head swim! Technical analysts, or chartists, also care about flags, pennants, candlesticks, cup-and-handle, and head-and-shoulders patterns.

But they don't care about financial reports, company sales and earnings, products, or, for that matter, even company names! A chart is the only source of information deemed relevant, so there is no need to read all that fine print in financial statements. Sounds too good to be true? Well, I think it is.

Technical analysis predicts the future direction of security prices based on past market data. It evokes either love-it or hate-it reactions from most people. It has several critics, from the side of academics and fundamental analysis. Peter Lynch said, "Charts are great for predicting the past." Warren Buffett said, "If past history was all there was to the game, the richest people would be librarians." Yet no other area of investment analysis has such dedicated supporters. Many books are written on the subject. I am guessing its followers must be averse to studying financial reports—it is definitely more tedious than plotting a few indicators over a chart on your favorite website.

Many years ago, I attended a stock-trading seminar. The presenter said that he set himself a lifetime goal to figure out which indicators actually work for predicting stock movements, studied hundreds of them over several years and finally came up with a solution. "Here is what I want you to do," he said. "Draw a 21-day this indicator, and a 15-day that oscillator, and superimpose them with trade volume. If all trend upwards, there is your buy signal. But, even if that indeed worked reliably in the past, where is the guarantee it continues to work in the future? Given the wealth of data available, one could always find patterns that worked for certain periods in the past, only to see them break down later.

Another seminar touted a "completely automated stock screening tool that uses sophisticated pattern analysis." It flashed "instant buy alerts" with green arrows and "sell alerts" with red arrows. I always wonder why the creators of such a wonderful tool try to sell it for $99.95 instead of using it and trading themselves a fortune.

Consider one of the most common technical analysis tools, trend lines with support and resistance. If you draw a line between daily low prices of a stock, and another line between daily high prices, quite often these lines will be nearly parallel. If both lines point up, then the stock price is increasing, and vice versa. The lower line is called support; the upper line is resistance. And, once such a trend is established, the stock is considered likely to stay in the channel between support and resistance lines.

Does this sound reasonable? Many would agree, but think about the following analogy. Let's say it snowed Monday through Wednesday and was clear the rest of the week for two weeks in a row. Do you think it is going to snow Monday through Wednesday the following week as well? Now are you sure that stock will stay in the channel?

Market timing and technical analysis go hand-in-hand, and there is no credible evidence that either technique is viable. The attraction of technical analysis is that it can create a trade recommendation fairly easily, but don't you believe it. Do your research, do your homework, and leave head-and-shoulder patterns to chartists.

Rule

39 Avoid Frequent Trading

Day trading is not investing, it is gambling.

If a buy-and-hold approach doesn't appear to work well enough, or is suffering through a bear market, the temptation to trade often to take advantage of stock price fluctuations on a monthly, weekly, or even daily basis is very strong. If you could only buy near the bottom and sell near the top, you could make a very handsome living and eliminate the need for your regular day job.

That is exactly what my friend Dave thought when he got a taste of success in day trading. The time was early 2000, and technology stocks were on fire. Dave's strategy was to place a large number of limit orders to buy just after the market opened, and wait until a few of them were executed (for a total amount that he was comfortable with). After that, he canceled the remaining orders, and placed sell orders at slightly higher prices for the stocks that he had bought earlier. He would then profit from the fluctuations. And this strategy worked quite well for some time. He was making several thousand dollars a day on the average, and was considering quitting his job.

March 31, 2000, was one the first big down days on the Nasdaq market. The Nasdaq dropped 350 points that day in very heavy trading. Dave saw this and attempted to cancel his limit orders, but he couldn't get through to the brokerage. Phone lines were busy and internet traffic was very heavy, so he couldn't log on either. Thinking that he might have a better chance at work because he had a faster internet connection there, he rushed to his office as fast as he could. When he arrived 30 minutes later, he found that all of his limit orders have been executed, and the average stock dropped by nearly 10% after that. The broker issued a margin call, and Dave was afraid he could lose his house. Thankfully, it didn't come to that, but he did lose all the profits he earned in previous months and an additional $50,000 of his principal. In just one day.

While one could argue that Dave's strategy was flawed, it nevertheless illustrates the dangers of day trading. I am certain that there are successful day traders who can make a consistent living out of it, just as there are successful blackjack or poker players and race horse bettors. To me, day trading is very similar to those occupations. It is not investing; it is gambling.

In addition to poor odds (by far, most day traders lose money), day traders accumulate commission costs—and if you make several trades a day, these costs add up quickly. They are also subject to unfavorable tax treatment—they incur a high short-term gains rate if they make money, and yet you can deduct only a total of $3,000 per year. And they support a number of accountants, as all those trades need to be recorded and reported to the IRS.

In 2001, a couple from Florida decided to form a business out of their day trading operations, and attempted to declare their losses from trading as regular business losses. The tax court disagreed, and they were stuck with a huge tax bill, in addition to losing money from their trading activities.

Finally, a day trader needs to spend a number of hours per day sitting in front of a computer screen staring at stock prices, charts and patterns. What a waste of a life! You deserve better than that. Resist the lure of a thriving day trader, because for every success there are countless failures.

40 Be Aware of the Rules of the Street

Take well-known Wall Street sayings with a grain of salt.

Throughout this book, I presented a number of rules that I believe are instrumental in achieving good investment returns. There are also many unwritten rules on Wall Street, and some are so well known that they became proverbs. Does it make sense to follow them? Let's examine the most famous ones.

Let Your Winners Run. This rule states that it is better to keep your winning stocks as opposed to taking profits after a stock reaches a certain price point, or after realizing some percentage gain. Generally, this is a good rule to follow—often, most of a portfolio's return is realized from gains from a few super-performing stocks. But, as always, re-evaluate your stocks and sell because fundamentals changed, not because of the stock price variations.

Cut Your Losers Short. It is the opposite of the previous adage, and it advocates minimizing your losses. Many people use this rule automatically by setting stop-loss orders to sell if the stock drops by, for example, 15% or 20%. However, due to stock fluctuations, it often simply means that you are planning to sell a stock for 20% less than you paid for it—hardly a recipe for a good return. If the stock deserves to be sold (and that could well be the case for many losers), then by all the means sell it, but don't base it on price variations.

The Trend Is Your Friend. This is probably the most important rule for technical analysis followers. Simply put, it states that a stock is likely to continue its current price trend. As explained in Rules 9 and 36, trying to predict future prices based on the past doesn't pay. However, since there are so many traders and looking at the trend is possibly their first priority, trends often do continue for some time until the fundamentals inevitably catch up to the stock price.

Don't Catch a Falling Knife. This rule is a variation of the previous proverb, and it warns against buying shares of a declining stock. It makes sense to pay attention to this one, since declining stocks frequently sport very attractive valuation metrics (such as P/E ratio) and thus appear to be bargains, especially compared to the prices they fetched recently. Sometimes they are, but quite often there is a good reason why a stock is dropping. As always, don't buy because the price is low, but evaluate it based on its future prospects.

A Rising Tide Lifts All Boats. This one implies that a rising market will help all stocks to advance as well. As far as overall investor sentiment is concerned, that is probably true. However, as discussed in Rule 27, the "market" doesn't move individual stocks; it is the other way around. There are always stinkers in the best market as well as advancers in the worst environment.

Sell in May and Go Away. It is an example of many seasonal anomalies that sometimes affect market performance. This particular adage predicts relatively poor market performance during summer, linked, perhaps, to summer vacations taken by investment bankers and most of Europe. You may have also heard of the January Effect, the September Effect, Santa Claus Rally, and others. While there is some historical evidence to back up these "strategies," the calendar-related returns do not always occur, and as more investors become aware of them, their effect diminishes or disappears altogether.

Buy Low, Sell High. This one is, of course, the most famous, as well as the most useless saying. All of us will be well-advised to follow this rule, but, unfortunately, it doesn't explain just how to go about it. Why I am not surprised? I can only suggest following your own rules consistently and they should help you in achieving your goals.

There are many other Wall Street sayings you may have heard. Take them with a grain of salt, and apply your own rules first in any situations.

41 Money Is Not the Goal

Investing is not all about money. If you enjoy the process and have fun, you will improve your chances of success.

Did you ever wonder what motivates super rich people, like Bill Gates or Michael Dell, to get up and go to work every day? They already have enough money to last them scores of lifetimes. The answer, of course, is that for them, their work is not about money, and it never was. Bill Gates didn't start Microsoft to become a multi-billionaire; he wanted to build a dominating software business. Money was never an explicit goal; it was a by-product of his activities.

Almost all successful individuals operate under the same principle. They enjoy their work; they live and breathe it their every spare moment. They are motivated by the process, not by the financial outcome. The financial rewards then usually follow automatically.

The investment process, even though it is obviously financial in its very nature, is no different. Successful investors never set monetary goals for themselves; rather, they enjoy the process of investing—searching for good companies, doing research, studying company reports, etc. For some this may appear dull, but not for them. If money were the motivating factor, they would have stopped investing quite early in their careers. If your goal were to achieve, for example, $1,000,000 in investable assets, what would you do once you reached that objective? Will you liquidate your holdings and go fishing, or will you continue investing?

Financial planners ask their clients about their income, expenses, tax situation, and a myriad other monetary details, run them through their software, and come up with a number. If you amass that number of dollars within an appropriate time interval, then you have good chances of being able to fund your retirement. Without a doubt, this calculation is important; I have done it and you should too. But knowing what your magic number is and even accumulating it is not what investing is all about. It is the process, not the destination, that is important. Even though I know what my number is, it has never been my goal. I plan to keep on investing for the rest of my life, because that is what I enjoy doing.

I am not saying that if you invest strictly out of necessity, or if you find investing boring and uninteresting, you will necessarily fail. But I do think that, as in other aspects of life, you are far more likely to succeed in investing if you enjoy the process and have fun along the way, too. And as a side effect, you will accumulate wealth. I find this outlook very invigorating. How about you?

42 These Are My Rules. What Are Yours?

Develop your own set of rules and follow them unflinchingly.

The rules presented in this book are obviously my rules. I have arrived at them after years of investing experience, learning from my mistakes, and making numerous improvements and adjustments in the process. They served me well in the past and I am certain will continue to do so in the future. But this does not necessarily mean that they will serve you just as well.

Many conclusions I made in this book could be considered controversial. I recognize and accept that. For example, I expressed strongly negative views about technical analysis and day trading. They never worked for me, but this doesn't mean I claim that no one can succeed using these techniques. In fact, I am sure that many people are employing these strategies to their advantage. The point is, develop your own set of rules based on your individual investing style and experience. Write these rules down and believe in them. Once you do, follow your own system consistently. Second-guessing it for any reason will inevitably lead to regrets later.

So, what are your rules?

A Bibliography

Damodaran, Aswath. *Investment Fables*.
Prentice Hall Books.
ISBN-10: 0-13-140312-5
ISBN-13: 978-0131403123

Gardner, David and, Tom. *The Motley Fool Investment Guide*. Fireside.
ISBN-10: 0-7432-0174-4
ISBN-13: 978-0743201742

Greenblatt, Joel. *You Can Be a Stock Market Genius*. Fireside.
ISBN-10: 0-6848-4007-3
ISBN-13: 978-0684840079

Lynch, Peter. *One Up on Wall Street*. Fireside.
ISBN-10: 0-7432-0040-3
ISBN-13: 978-0743200400

Lynch, Peter. *Beating the Street*. Fireside.
ISBN-10: 0-6718-9163-4
ISBN-13: 978-0671891633

Siegel, Jeremy. *Stocks for the Long Run*.
McGraw-Hill Professional.
ISBN-10: 0-0714-9470-7
ISBN-13: 978-0071494700

Zweig, Jason. *Your Money and Your Brain*.
Simon & Schuster.
ISBN-10: 0-7432-7668-X
ISBN-13: 978-0-7432-7668-9

B Internet Resources

1. http://finance.yahoo.com/
   Market news, detailed information on stocks, quotes, etc.

2. http://www.fool.com/
   News, tutorials on investment topics, stock recommendations

3. http://www.j3sg.com/
   Information on insider activity

4. http://www.888options.com/
   Good summaries of various options strategies

C Glossary

Accredited (Qualified) Investor	A high net worth individual or entity that can invest into hedge funds. Needs to have at least $1million in net worth, or have an annual income of $200K if single or $300K jointly if married.
Bear Market	A declining market that drops at least 20% from peak to trough.
Bond	A promissory note issued by a company or government to repay the principal plus interest for a specified period of time.
Bull Market	An advancing market.
Call Option	A contract that gives the buyer the right, but not the obligation, to buy an underlying security at the strike price before or on the expiration date.
Capital Gain (Loss)	Profit (loss) from sale of an investment.
Compound Interest	A way interest accrues over time.
Correction	A drop of at least 10% in the market from peak to trough.
Covered Call Strategy	A strategy to sell call options while owning the underlying stock.
Diversification	Spreading investments among different securities or different investment types.

EBITDA	Earnings before interest, taxes, depreciation, and amortization.
Exercise	An act of an option buyer to use his right to buy or sell an underlying stock at the strike price.
Expense Ratio	A percentage of invested assets that a mutual fund charges for its services.
Expiration Date	The date an option ceases to exist.
Fundamental Research	Analysis of companies based on financial metrics, such as sales, earnings, assets, etc.
Hedge Fund	A type of mutual fund that is not regulated by the SEC and is usually available only to accredited investors.
Hedging	A technique that acts as an insurance against possible market losses.
In the Money	Option contract where the strike price is above the current stock market price for calls, and below the market price for puts.
IRA	Individual Retirement Account.
Leverage	Ability to control a certain amount of investments by committing only a fraction of the funds required to purchase these investments.
Limit Order	An order to buy or sell a security at a specified price.
Load	A charge, expressed in percentage of invested assets, that a mutual fund may charge for buying (front load) or selling (back load) its shares.
Lock In Period	A time interval, imposed by some hedge funds, when an investor is unable to sell his position in the fund.
Margin Account	An account type that permits the account holder to borrow funds from the brokerage with existing securities and cash as collateral for the loan.

Margin Call	A demand upon an account holder to deposit additional cash or securities to maintain margin requirements.
Market Capitalization	Total market value of a security, calculated by multiplying stock price by the number of shares outstanding.
Market Order	An order to buy or sell a security at the current price.
Mutual Fund	An investment company that pools together investors' funds and makes investment decisions on their behalf.
Option Premium	Cost of options contract.
Out of the Money	Option contract where the strike price is below the current stock market price for calls, and above the market price for puts.
P/E Ratio (Price to Earnings Ratio)	Price of stock divided by earnings per share over a one-year period.
PEG Ratio	P/E Ratio divided by stock earnings growth rate.
Penny Stocks	Low priced issues, usually below $1, very often highly speculative.
Put Option	A contract that gives the buyer the right, but not the obligation, to sell an underlying security at the strike price before or on the expiration date.
P/S Ratio (Price to Sales Ratio)	Price of stock divided by sales per share over a one-year period.
Qualified Investor	*See* **Accredited Investor**.
SEC	Securities and Exchange Commission.
Short Selling	Transactions where one borrows a security from a broker and immediately sells it, hoping it will go down in price so that one can profit by buying it back at a lower price and returning it to the broker.

Stop Loss Order	An order to sell a stock if it drops below a specified price.
Strike Price	A price at which an option can be exercised.
Technical Analysis	Analysis of markets and stocks based on past price movements, charts, trends, etc.
Treasury Bill	A short-term bond issued by the U.S. government.

About the Author

Leon Shirman earned his Ph.D. in Applied Mathematics from the University of California at Berkeley in 1990. He turned his attention to investing in 1987, after a market crash that year. In 2011, he earned Chartered Financial Analyst (CFA) designation. He is now the Managing Partner of his investment company, Emerald Hills Capital.

Prior to launching his investment career, Shirman worked in prominent high-tech companies, such as Sun Microsystems and Microsoft, and in start-ups, including one he founded. His research has yielded a number of publications in scientific magazines, as well as numerous U.S. patents.

Shirman lives in Redwood City, California with his wife and two daughters.

42 Rules Program

A lot of people would like to write a book, but only a few actually do. Finding a publisher, and distributing and marketing the book are challenges that prevent even the most ambitious authors from getting started.

If you want to be a successful author, we'll provide you the tools to help make it happen. Start today by completing a book proposal at our website http://42rules.com/write/.

For more information, email info@superstarpress.com or call 408-257-3000.

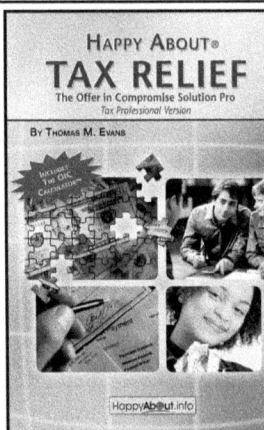

A Message From Super Star Press™

Thank you for your purchase of this 42 Rules Series book. It is available online at:
http://www.happyabout.com/42rules/sensible-investing.php or at other online and physical bookstores. To learn more about contributing to books in the 42 Rules series, check out **http://superstarpress.com**.

Please contact us for quantity discounts at **sales@superstarpress.com**.

If you want to be informed by email of upcoming books, please email **bookupdate@superstarpress.com**.